SPA®K

The Insight to Growing Brands

SPA®K

THE INSIGHT TO GROWING BRANDS

PADDY RANGAPPA

SIMON & SCHUSTER

London · New York · Sydney · Toronto · New Delhi

A CBS COMPANY

First published in India by Simon & Schuster India, 2017
A CBS company

1 3 5 7 9 10 8 6 4 2

Simon & Schuster India
818, Indraprakash Building,
21, Barakhamba Road,
New Delhi 110001

www.simonandschuster.co.in

Simon & Schuster UK, London
Simon & Schuster Australia, Sydney

Hardback ISBN: 978-81-933552-2-0
eBook ISBN: 978-81-933552-3-7

Typeset in India by Manipal Digital Systems Pvt. Ltd.
Printed and bound in India by Replika Press Pvt. Ltd.

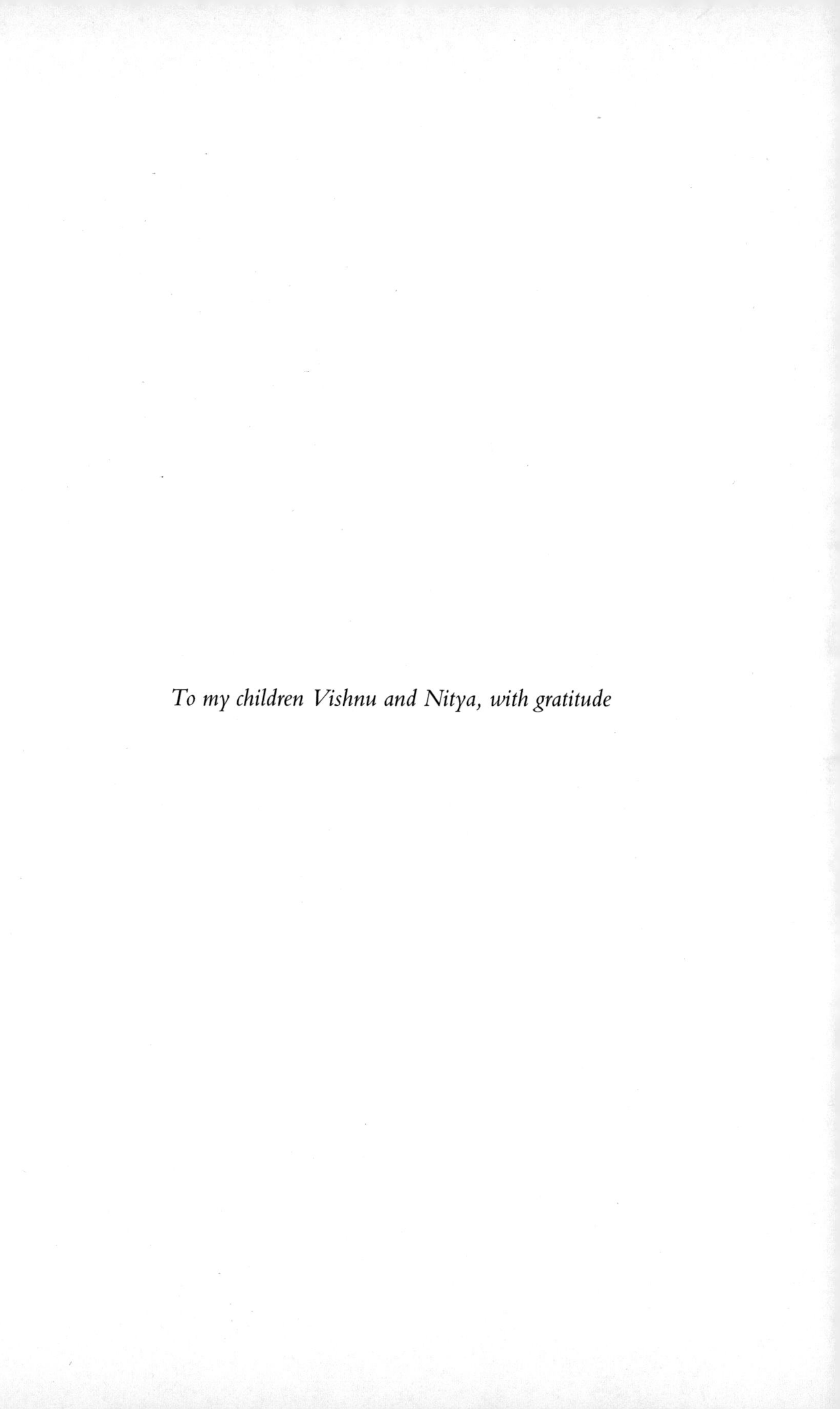

To my children Vishnu and Nitya, with gratitude

Table of Contents

Introduction

'Life consists not in holding good cards but about playing those you hold well.'
—Josh Billings

Many people believe that good advertising can evoke emotions—joy, sorrow, laughter and, sometimes, a combination of these responses—and they're right. But that's not the reason you should pursue good advertising. You should do it because it can generate long-term profitable growth for your brand! And *that* is the reason for this book.

Put simply, this book is about how you can grow your brand by making an emotional connection with people through relevant consumer insights and using these insights in your brand strategy and advertising. Doing this well has never been more important.

In the highly competitive and fragmented markets of today, where countless brands vie for the business of time-strapped, super-busy, and digitally hyper-connected consumers, generating long-term growth is particularly challenging. You need a product that works, that is priced right, that is well-distributed, and so on—but equally, since these alone will not guarantee growth, you need to build a brand.

The book is less about the 'what' and more about the 'how'; it's more a practitioner's handbook than a research study, more manual than textbook. By practising the techniques presented in it, you will learn *how* to find insights for your brand and, having found them, *how* to develop powerful advertising to bring these insights to life, in partnership with your advertising agency.

How the Book Is Structured

Before delving into the *how* you need some perspective on the *why*—not so much to appreciate the theory, but simply to imbibe the faith that the pursuit of insights is worthwhile. Part One of the book—'The Insight to Growing Brands'—is about the challenges facing a brand in today's competitive world. If consumers, with their digital devices, social connections, work priorities, and family commitments, have little time for brands, how can a brand grow? I consider some commonly held beliefs about brand growth and show—through evidence across many countries and categories—why focusing on heavy users, targeting usage instead of reach, and relying on short-term promotions are all wrong. I then hone in on how a brand can grow by considering two simple ideas—physical availability and mental availability. Physical availability is simply being present and available when consumers are shopping. Mental availability is being on consumers' minds when they're shopping. Among the hundreds of brands physically available when they shop, consumers only consider the few that they know and remember—if your brand is not mentally available, it will not be chosen, as simple as that (Sharp, 2010 and Romaniuk, 2016).

Obviously your brand needs both. But the rest of the book focuses on increasing your brand's *mental availability* by making the right emotional connection with consumers (and leaves the important topic of physical availability to experts in the field of distribution and sales).

Part Two, 'The Insight to Connecting with Consumers', focuses on the term 'insight'—what it is, how to recognize it, and, most importantly, how to develop it. You will learn how to generate insights with the right team of people, using a simple step-by-step process—starting with the key business challenge that your brand faces. There are numerous examples—real and hypothetical—that will help illustrate the lessons.

Once you have a powerful insight that everyone in the team believes in, you will learn how to make the insight pivotal to your brand strategy and influence your marketing plans, especially the advertising.

Part Three of the book—'Creativity That Drives Brand Growth'—shows how to develop great advertising through 'CRAFT'—through unwavering 'Conviction', channelizing the right 'Resources', employing a robust, practical 'Approach' or process, building a strong 'Foundation', and bringing all this together through 'Teamwork' and collaboration with the advertising agency. CRAFT is an acronym for age-old principles for developing great advertising. Since many of these principles are left by the wayside when business leaders get caught up in activity that generates, at best, temporary blips in a gloomy sales trend, Part Three offers an alternative—one that will put a brand on a long-term growth trajectory.

How This Book Is Different

While researching for this book I was struck by two discoveries, both very heartening.

The first relates to Part Two of this book. Not much has been written on the topic of consumer insights. While there are references to the role of insights in advertising, and how to recognize an insight, there is no literature on *developing* insights. This book fills that crucial gap.

The second point concerns Part Three. Most books on creative campaigns and advertising are written by advertising practitioners and contain entertaining anecdotes about how great campaigns have built great brands. And while they are an interesting read for people in advertising, if you're a marketing executive, these books offer little help on how to inspire great advertising from your agency partners, how to provide them with direction, and how to recognize brilliance in the creative work they bring you. These are the precise areas covered in this book.

In other words, this book is structured not just for the marketing professional, but also for the broader marketing team working on insights and advertising.

Since the ad agency is an important part of this team, the book is useful for advertising executives as well. It will help them appreciate the client's point of view, making them better team players in the exciting advertising journey of the brand.

Finally the book is a useful read for those interested in marketing and advertising as it demystifies what is often seen as an esoteric subject. While readers may not use the processes described to actually develop advertisements, they will find that the book helps them appreciate (or criticize!) the advertising they come across.

A Word of Caution

I'd like to offer three points of advice to the reader interested in using the lessons from this book.

First, finding an insight alone does not guarantee business success. You need to use the insight to shape your brand strategy and advertising; in other words, you need to bet your marketing on it. Put your money where your mouth is and you will reap the rewards.

Second, simply reading the book will not translate into creative ideas. You will need to practise the skills and techniques you've learnt. But it's an enjoyable process! Even advertising sceptics acknowledge that advertising is fun!

And finally, following CRAFT's principles will not lead you to brilliant creative campaigns every time. Creativity is an art that is ultimately judged by the consumer. Advertising is not dissimilar to making a movie. Even Steven Spielberg doesn't deliver box-office hits every time. But—and this is what makes all the difference—he delivers them more often than the average film-maker. Likewise, following the principles of CRAFT will increase the probability of producing brilliant creative, and therefore you will produce it more often.

PART ONE

The Insight to Growing Brands

Chapter 1
Brand Growth: Challenging Times

'If you can find a path with no obstacles, it probably doesn't lead anywhere.'
—Frank A. Clark

The pursuit of profitable growth unites brands regardless of their size, cost or nature. Yet this pursuit has never been more challenging. Understanding the reasons for these challenges will shed some light on how to overcome them.

We live in an era of brand proliferation, with every market fragmented and crammed with brands. Consumers are not just spoiled for choice, they are befuddled. Figure 1.1 shows the extent of brand proliferation between 1970 and 2012 in the USA alone. If you wanted sports shoes in 1970 you had a choice of 5 items; in 1998 you could select from 285, and by 2012, there were over 3,000 options vying for your attention!

We're also in the midst of a difficult economic period. Over the last few years, global GDP (gross domestic product) growth has slowed to between 2 and 3 per cent annually; many consumer categories are flat or declining. War, terrorism, and natural disasters are adding to economic woes. Under such circumstances, brand growth is under pressure.

Figure 1.1 Trend in Product Variety (Number of Models) for Some Products in the USA

Product	1970	1998	2012
Automobile models	140	260	684
Newspapers	339	790	>5,000
TV screens (size)	5	15	43
Movies (at the cinema)	267	458	1,410
Breakfast cereals	160	340	4,945
Milk	4	19	>50
Mouthwash	15	66	223
Sports shoes	5	285	3,371
Mineral water	16	50	195
Tights	5	90	594

Source: Cox, M.W.; Alm, R. (1998, revised 2013); 'The Right Stuff: America's Move to Mass Customisation'; *Annual Report of Federal Reserve Bank of Dallas.*

Lastly, we're in the digital era. The explosion in the use of the internet through personal computers in the early 2000s, and recently through smartphones, has transformed consumer behaviour. The website Internet Live Stats[1] estimates, as of December 2016, that of the 7.4 billion people on earth, an estimated 3.5 billion have access to over 1.1 billion websites on the internet today. A recent study (Salesforce, 2014) showed that 85 per cent of consumers believe the mobile phone is an integral part of their lives and spend an average of 3.3 hours per day on it. A large ten-city survey reveals that 79 per cent of smartphone users reach for their phones within 15 minutes of waking up (Adweek, 2013).

Unsurprisingly, this digital explosion has made the lives of already busy consumers ridiculously hectic. Consider the things that have always kept people preoccupied: working, playing, exercising, spending time with the family, and maintaining social connections. But today, consumers are doing all of that *while* being digitally engaged—sharing information, shopping, playing games, browsing, and so on. To capture the attention of such distracted

1 You can visit the website at <www.internetlivestats.com>, accessed on 21 December 2016.

consumers is extremely difficult for any brand (especially when it is competing with hundreds of brands trying to do the same thing).

The Decline of Mass Marketing and Advertising

From a marketing point of view, one could say that the 1980s and 1990s were the advertising decades. This was the time when big brands invested in brilliant advertising, which in turn made them bigger. In this period advertising evolved from communicating a simple, functional benefit—'washes whiter', 'fits better' or 'lasts longer'—to appealing to the consumer's emotions. For example, the Procter & Gamble (P&G) deodorant Sure, instead of talking about long-lasting protection, challenged you to 'raise your hand if you're sure' through an engaging, musical television advertisement showing people in different, physically demanding situations raising their hands with confidence.[2]

The 1980s and 90s, consequently, were a heady time for the advertising industry. As Ian Leslie, a veteran ad man and writer (Leslie, 2015), puts it, 'We made famous stuff, and we made stuff famous. Every ad in the Levi's campaign, for instance, with its combustible blend of sex, music and Americana, was a national event.'

While being a sensational time for the ad agency, it was a worrisome time for the marketing company, typified by its Scrooge-like finance director. First, the enormous amount of money spent on advertising was viewed as wasteful and excessive. When an after-shave brand advertised on the TV show *Friends,* for example, it reached a large section of its target audience. But *Friends* was also viewed by thousands of men not interested in buying an after-shave in the near future (as well as thousands of women unlikely to ever be interested in buying an after-shave!)—so the brand was paying to reach people it didn't need. Second, most companies did not employ sophisticated advertising testing

---

2 You can watch the deodorant Sure's commercial on YouTube, at <https://www.youtube.com/watch?v=t-FZ21uDKeQ>, accessed on 21 November 2016.

and post-advertising tracking, and so were never sure about the impact of this massive expenditure.

With the advent of digital media and their ability to target end users precisely and measure results easily, companies have begun viewing creative TV campaigns as inefficient, wasteful, and even primitive. Digital marketing has made it very easy for marketers to reach the right consumers—exactly the ones they want—for example, the ones who have shown an interest in, or have purchased, their brand. Even as consumers are looking for information on a product category or searching for something related, marketers get precise data—they count how many people saw the message ('impressions'), how many of those who saw it clicked through to get more information, and, in some cases, how many of the clickers actually bought the brand. With the help of this framework, the after-shave brand cited above could target potential as well as existing users close to when they're thinking of buying an after-shave. Company executives might argue that they could keep such loyal fans of the brands engaged through a website and social media platforms, where the brand could have interesting two-way, tailored dialogues with consumers.

The digital medium has also made it possible to sell directly to consumers. Through e-commerce, people can click their way to purchases without visiting a physical store.

In fact, the digital medium seems to align itself with—and indeed, bolster—some commonly held perceptions about consumers and brands.

Commonly Held Perceptions about Consumers, Brands, and Brand Growth

Here are five impressions about consumers, brands, and brand growth.

1. **People are rational.** Consumers evaluate brands carefully. They believe these brands are different from each other and remain steadfastly loyal to their favourite brands.

2. **Brand growth comes from getting heavy and loyal consumers to use more.** Light and very light users who buy a brand infrequently don't matter. And retention (of existing customers) is cheaper than acquisition.

3. **Brand growth can come not only by expanding the number of users (reach), but also by increasing usage (buying frequency).** A small brand can hope to have higher usage than the market leader.

4. **Long-term growth can be generated by a series of discrete short-term activities.** Retail brands need monthly promotions to draw consumers in and boost sales. Temporary price-discount promotions attract non-users, who, having tried the product, will be induced to buy it again, thereby generating incremental long-term sales.

5. **With digital evolution, mass marketing is dying.** Brands should divert precious funding from marketing to e-commerce and other digital platforms to drive brand growth.

I've heard different versions of these statements uttered with conviction, as if they were the absolute truth. And for these reasons, many brands are increasingly focusing on loyal consumers, investing in brand engagement through social media, doubling up on e-commerce, and reducing their investment in classical brand advertising.

Unfortunately, **all these statements are false**. The next chapter will show you why, and also explain the real source of brand growth.

SUMMARY

- Brands today face many challenges on their path to achieving profitable growth. They operate in highly competitive markets, often in precarious economic conditions. And they have to reach consumers who are very busy and spend a lot of time engaging with the digital medium.

- In response to this, and because of a few commonly-held beliefs, marketers are moving away from classical advertising and mass marketing, investing instead in programmes focused on loyalty, retention, e-commerce, and brand engagement. But these beliefs are false! So basing decisions on them is wrong.

Chapter 2
Consumers and Brands: Myth and Reality

'Stubbornness does have its helpful features. You always know what you are going to be thinking tomorrow.'
—Glen Beaman

Proof that the five core beliefs described in the previous chapter about consumers, brands, and brand growth are myths is offered by robust research in the area of social psychology by experts like Daniel Kahneman and Jonathan Haidt, and by the researchers at the Ehrenberg-Bass Institute of Marketing Science.

People Are Rational

The belief that people are logical creatures leads to the conviction that, as consumers, they spend time thinking about and evaluating brands carefully.

Unfortunately, we are not as rational as we think we are or want to be. In his brilliant book *Thinking, Fast and Slow,* Daniel Kahneman explains how all of us have two systems of thinking. System 1 is automatic, intuitive, quick, and emotional. We use it with little effort; indeed it operates on its own and often without our knowledge. System 2 is logical, reasoned, and rational. We use it to make assessments and decisions (Kahneman, 2011). The surprising thing is not the existence of two systems but the fact that it is the intuitive System 1 that dominates our thinking. If we were to borrow an analogy from films, System 1 is the conquering hero, while System 2 is the helpful, but often ignored, sidekick.

In *The Righteous Mind: Why Good People Are Divided by Religion and Politics,* Jonathan Haidt offers compelling insights into this area. He explains that intuition always come first, strategic reasoning second. Often we use strategic reasoning (Kahneman's System 2) to justify our already-held intuitive, preconditioned beliefs (Kahneman's System 1). Haidt draws the analogy of the rider (logic and reasoning), trying to control the elephant he is on (intuition and emotion), but only being able to do it to the extent that the elephant *wants* to be controlled. When the elephant turns right, for example, the rider quickly steers the elephant to move to the right. In other words we use reasoning and logic (constituting about 1 per cent of our thinking) to justify—often, and on the fly—our pre-held views (the other 99 per cent).

How does this relate to brands? Well, if we rely on intuitive thinking for the big issues that we face in the realms of religion, politics and morals, it is wildly unrealistic to imagine that we would use reasoning and logic to select brands. After all, choosing which toothpaste to buy is a trivial decision, much more likely to be handled by our hyperactive, always-on System 1—our elephant.

Evidence supports this. Talking about how we choose brands (Romaniuk, 2016), Jenni Romaniuk says:

> The thoughts and actions of buying are typically these:
>
> - instantaneous, without (much) conscious deliberation
> - influenced by context, which defines which part of memory is triggered
> - inconsistent, in that today's retrieved thoughts are not necessarily retrieved tomorrow.

She then talks about how we use 'cued retrieval' based on the external environment (for example, the desire to consume a soft drink when outside on a hot day), which facilitates a quick, intuitive decision. In another study (Romaniuk, Sharp, and Ehrenberg, 2007), Romaniuk concludes that:

> [. . .] brand choice is a relatively trivial task compared with deciding whether or not to buy from the product category.

> So buyers seldom spend much time comparing brands in the category, and as such, differentiation (which is relative to other brands) is not given much attention.

To prove the point, the study measured the extent to which current brand users across 17 categories (including spirits, supermarkets, and fast food) in Australia and the UK believed each brand in the category (for example Coca-Cola, Diet Coke, Pepsi-Cola, Fanta, Pepsi Max, Schweppes, and Canada Dry in soft drinks) was perceived to be distinct from the others. The detailed findings for each brand are reported in the study but Figure 2.1 is a summary, showing the average score for each category in the two countries.

Figure 2.1 Perceived Difference or Uniqueness of Brands in 17 Categories across Australia and the UK, 2005

	Current users perceiving it is different⋆ (%)	**Current users perceiving it is unique⋆ (%)**	**Current users perceiving it is either⋆ (%)**
Spirits (Aus)	20	27	36
Supermarkets (Aus)	25	21	31
Skincare (Aus)	17	21	30
Ice cream (UK)	14	11	20
Fast food (Aus)	16	13	20
Banking (UK)	13	10	18
Soft drinks (UK)	9	9	16
Condiments (UK)	10	9	17
F&V drinks (UK)	11	8	16
Ready sauces (UK)	9	7	14
Computers (UK)	9	10	14
Soups (UK)	8	5	12
Yoghurt (UK)	8	5	11
Cars (Aus)	9	6	11
Cars (UK)	8	6	11
Water (UK)	6	6	10
Electronics (UK)	4	6	8
Average (all 17)	**11**	**10**	**17**

⋆average score of all brands in each category

Source: Romaniuk, Jenni; Sharp, Byron; Ehrenberg, Andrew (2007); 'Evidence Concerning the Importance of Perceived Brand Differentiation'; *Australasian Marketing Journal*; Vol 15.

This table shows quite clearly that consumers of a brand do not choose it because they believe it's different or unique. At the point of purchase they make the decision based on the brands they *remember*—mental availability—and can *find easily*—physical availability (Sharp, 2010).

Brand Growth Comes from Getting Heavy and Loyal Consumers to Use More

A corollary to this belief is that light users should be ignored. And that retention of existing consumers is cheaper than the acquisition of new ones.

Again, false!

Much marketing attention, as well as dollars, is invested in brands under the assumption that converting heavy users into brand loyalists ensures rapid growth and market dominance. However research proves that heavy users of the category hardly ever restrict their purchases to one brand. For example, in the soft drinks category in Mexico and Turkey, less than 1 per cent of the heaviest users—people who buy a soft drink once a day or more often—display sole brand loyalty to any one brand. Similarly, less than 1 per cent of the not-so-heavy users—those who buy a soft drink every two or three days—restrict their purchases to a single brand. The percentage of users who buy a single brand rises to 14 per cent in Turkey and 20 per cent in Mexico among light users—consumers who buy a soft drink twice or thrice a month—and to as high as 40 per cent in Turkey and 33 per cent in Mexico among the lightest users, people who buy a soft drink less than once a month (Romaniuk, 2016). In other words, there is some display of loyalty among the lightest category users (but this is most likely not because they love a particular brand but because they make such few purchases that the chance of these purchases being of a single brand increases). In any case, irrespective of whether passion or probability drives the behaviour, such users account for a very low volume.

The fact that heavy users cannot be the source of expansion is reemphasized in Figure 2.2. Among cola drinkers in the UK, the average buying frequency of Coca-Cola is 12 bottles a year. But very few cola users (around 3 per cent) buy Coca-Cola that often.

In fact, the bulk of them (about 80 per cent) buy it less than five times a year. The reason the average is 12 is that there are a few consumers who buy Coca-Cola very often, more than once a week. In order to expand, Coca-Cola cannot afford to ignore 80 per cent of its user base—the light and very light users. This is especially important because these users, by their very nature, buy the brand rarely and can therefore forget about it easily. While heavy users are important for Coca-Cola in terms of the volume they consume, they cannot be the source of growth. And being heavy users, they need few reminders about the brand, and any marketing aimed at light users will likely be seen and absorbed by them too.

Figure 2.2 Usage of Coca-Cola among Cola Drinkers in the UK, 2005

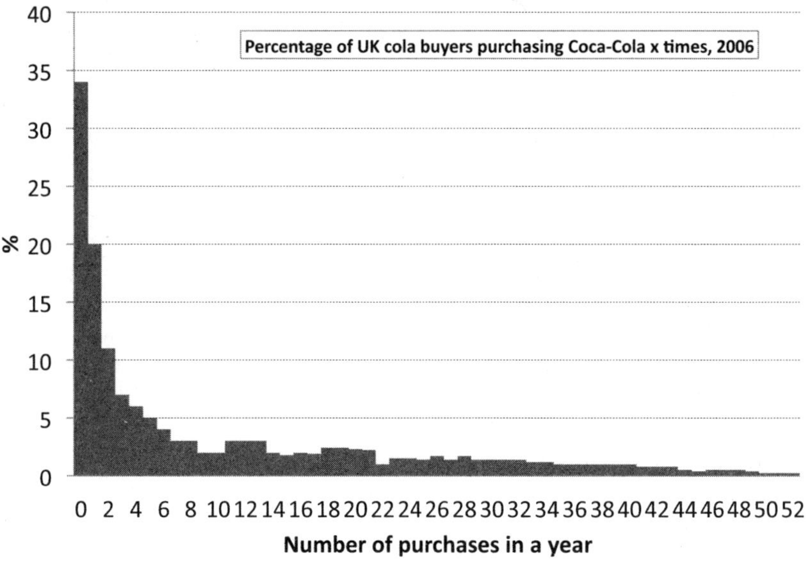

Source: Nielsen; quoted in Sharp, Byron and the researchers of the Ehrenberg-Bass Institute (2010); *How Brands Grow*.

Finally, retention is not cheaper than acquisition—as is often believed—because consumers naturally flit between brands. Chasing retention, or 100 per cent loyalty, is chasing a pipe dream. Consider Figure 2.3 for the automobile industry in the USA in 1998 (Terech, 2009). The market leader Ford enjoys the highest retention, or repeat purchase rate, of 64 per cent. But that still means 36 per cent of Ford users will defect from the brand. And things only get worse as you go down the list. In general, the smaller the brand, the higher the defection rate: 80 per cent of the smallest brand Plymouth's customers will buy a different car the next time and the number is only slightly lower, at approximately 70 per cent, for the next two small brands, Oldsmobile and Chrysler.

Figure 2.3 Retention and Defection for Automobile Brands in the USA, 1998-99

Brand	Market share (%)	Retention or repeat purchase (%)	Defection (%) (100-Retention)
Ford	25.3	64	36
Chevrolet	18.6	55	45
Dodge	11.1	48	52
Toyota	9.3	57	43
Honda	6.9	51	49
Nissan	4.3	39	61
Pontiac	4.1	30	70
Jeep	3.5	39	61
GMC	3.5	41	59
Mercury	3.2	36	64
Buick	3.1	41	59
Oldsmobile	2.5	29	71
Chrysler	2.4	33	67
Plymouth	2.3	20	80

Source: Terech, Andres; Bucklin, Randolph E.; Morrison, Donald G. (September 2009); 'Consideration, Choice and Classifying Loyalty'; *Marketing Letters*; 20.3.

If defection is inevitable, constantly acquiring customers (and re-acquiring them, as most customers oscillate between the few brands in their consideration set) is key, proving, once again, the indisputable importance of targeting all users, including (or especially) the light and very light users.

Brand Growth Can Come Not Only by Expanding the Number of Users (Reach), but Also by Increasing Usage (Buying Frequency)

Extending the logic of this statement, a smaller brand can hope to have higher usage than the market leader.

Unfortunately it cannot.

A small brand is subject to the harsh reality of double jeopardy. It loses out to the big brand on account of the number of people who use it (also called 'penetration' or 'reach') as well as the amount they use (also called 'usage' or 'buying frequency'). Figure 2.4 illustrates this for toothpaste brands in China for the year 2011. The biggest brand, Crest (market share 19 per cent), enjoys an annual penetration of 57 per cent and is purchased an average of 2.8 times a year by its customers. LSL, brand number five with a market share of 6 per cent, has a penetration of 23 per cent and an average annual buying rate of 2.2 times a year.

Figure 2.4 Market Share, Penetration, and Buying Rate for Toothpastes in China, 2011

Brand	Market share (%)	Penetration (%)	Buying rate (%)
Crest	19	57	2.8
Colgate	14	46	2.5
Zhonghua	12	43	2.4
Darlie	11	35	2.7
LSL	6	23	2.2

Source: Kantar Worldpanel China; quoted in Romaniuk, Jenni; Sharp, Byron (2016); *How Brands Grow: Part 2.*

Figure 2.5 shows the same data for detergent brands in the UK in 2005.

Figure 2.5 Market Share, Penetration, and Buying Rate for Detergents in the UK, 2005

Brand	Market share (%)	Penetration (%)	Buying rate (%)
Persil	22	41	3.9
Ariel	14	26	3.9
Bold	10	19	3.8
Daz	9	17	3.7
Surf	8	17	3.4

Source: Nielsen; quoted in Sharp, Byron (2010); *How Brands Grow.*

Clearly the opportunity for LSL in China and Surf in the UK is to grow penetration. If they succeed, they will automatically benefit with a modest growth in buying rate because the pattern of consumer behaviour rewards bigger brands with more purchases. Growing usage is akin to pushing water uphill. Both go against natural laws and will not succeed.

The belief that 'retention is cheaper than acquisition' has given an impetus to 'loyalty initiatives' geared to trying to sell more services to existing (loyal) consumers—we see this trend in banking, for example. But despite such efforts, the number of services customers have with each bank varies only a little, *and* this variation favours the bigger banks. For example (see Figure 2.6), the bigger banks in India, which have a much higher penetration, also have a slightly higher average number of products per customer.

Figure 2.6 Double Jeopardy in Banks in India, 2014

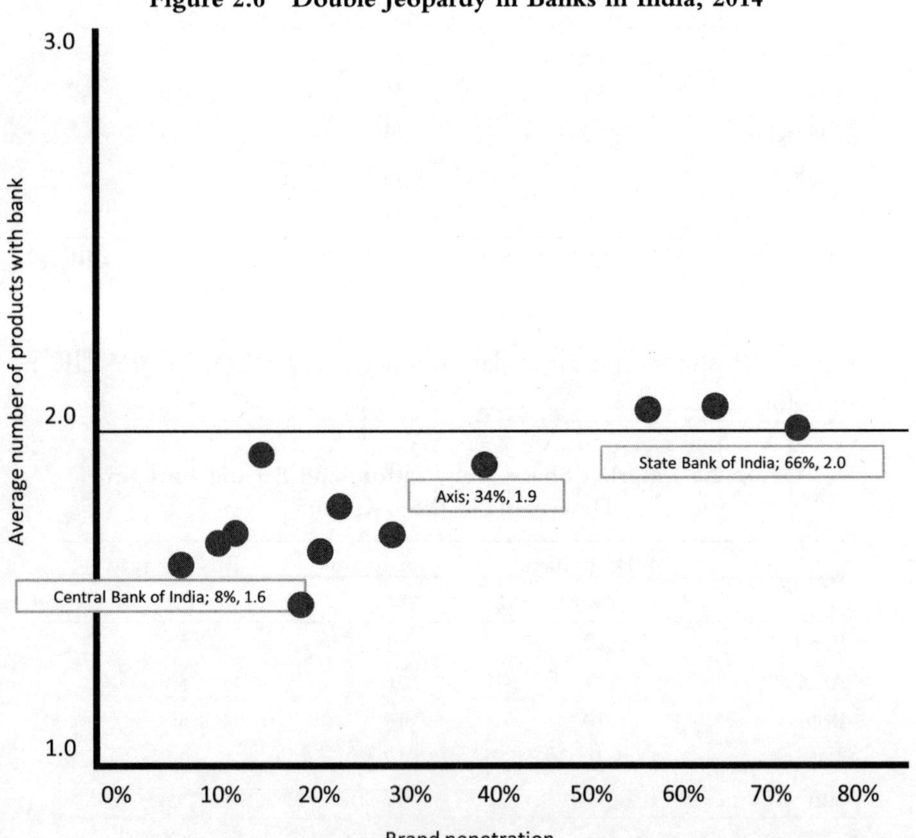

Source: Romaniuk, Jenni; Sharp, Byron (2016); *How Brands Grow: Part 2.*

Long-term Growth Can be Generated by a Series of Discrete Short-term Activities

Many brands, especially in retail, are so invested in this belief that their marketing consists almost entirely of a series of monthly promotions to bring consumers in and lift sales. Many also invest in periodic price-discount promotions hoping to attract non-users, who, by buying the brand subsequently will contribute to long-term growth.

Sadly, this is wishful thinking. Short-term promotions produce spikes in the month of the promotion, often at a lower profit margin if the promotion involves a price discount, but sales fall back after the promotion, doing nothing to the long-term trend. In Figure 2.7, the 'short-term promotions' line shows a flat long-term trend with spikes every month. In many cases, despite the spikes, the long-term trend could be downward. To get the brand on the 'long-term growth line' in the same chart requires a clear brand strategy and a series of programmes around this.

Figure 2.7 Hypothetical Example of Short-term Promotions

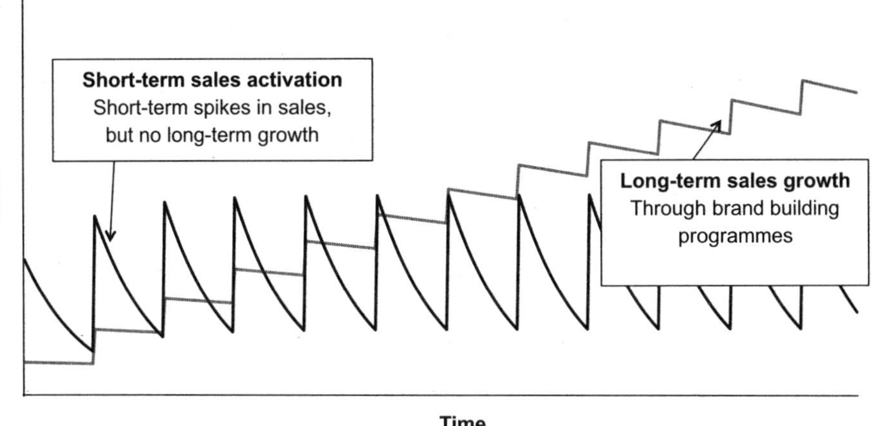

Another popular notion among business leaders and people involved in marketing and advertising is that there are two types of advertising—hard-hitting advertising with a promotional offer (usually an attractive price below the normal price available for a limited time) that boosts sales; and soft, emotional, brand advertising that builds brand image, equity, commitment, and loyalty, but not sales. This is wrong on both counts!

Let's start by looking at the impact of temporary price discounts. Before considering the evidence, let's briefly dwell on the profit impact of such a promotion. For simplicity let's assume the selling price of this hypothetical product is $100 and the direct cost of making it (material, packaging, direct labour, and so on) is $60. Then it enjoys a contribution margin (which is sales price less the direct cost) of $40 or 40 per cent. Now let's assume the price is dropped by 20 per cent during the promotion. Both are conservative assumptions: 40 per cent is a healthy contribution margin and it's safe to believe that you need at least a 20 per cent discount in price to attract significant extra purchases. The margin then would reduce to $20 (new price of $80 less cost of $60) which, expressed as a percentage of the selling price, is 25 per cent. Selling 10 units at full price generates a profit of $400 ($40 times 10). To make the same $400 during the promotion, the brand would need to sell 20 pieces (20 times $20). That is to say, sales would have to double for the brand to make the same profit as it did before the promotion.

Doubling the volume is a huge ask. But brands run promotions anyway, hoping that the temporary price discount will have a longer-term positive sales impact by attracting users of other brands and converting them into repeat-purchasers. Unfortunately, many studies show that this does not happen. For instance, a close examination of the sales impact of promotions of 25 packaged goods categories across four countries (Ehrenberg, Hammond, and Goodhardt, 1994) concluded that there is no long-term impact on sales induced by a short-term promotion. After the promotion-induced sales spike, sales settle roughly at the pre-promotion level. This is because:

1. The vast majority of people who availed of the promotion had bought that brand previously (80 per cent in the year before).

2. There is no change in their repeat buying rate after the promotion. In fact, the overall repeat purchase rate of all buyers remains surprisingly steady over the long haul, despite the many promotions that the brands indulge in at different times.

While such promotional campaigns don't work, when done well 'brand advertising' (a term to describe communication focused on the overall brand and not containing any short-term 'offer') generates positive sales growth in the 12-month period following the campaign. McDonald's has found, for example, that such brand advertising delivers a significantly higher return on investment (the incremental dollar sales generated by one dollar of advertising) than product or promotion content (quoted with permission from McDonald's).

In addition to this relatively longer term impact, many single-source, extended-period studies have measured the immediate impact of advertising. For example, John Philip Jones (Jones, 2015) demonstrates the impact of brand advertising in the week after. In his study, Jones found an average sales growth of 24 per cent in the first week after advertising across all brands, with the top 10 per cent brands registering a growth of 136 per cent and the bottom 10 per cent showing a decline of 27 per cent. The variation in performance is actually good news for marketers and agency managers. Not only is there strong empirical evidence to suggest that brand advertising works, but there's also proof that creativity matters. Jones identifies the three characteristics of ads that have the highest impact on sales:

1. They are intrinsically likeable.
2. They are visual, not verbal.
3. They are communicated in a way that's relevant to consumers.

Another study by Xueming Luo and Pieter J. de Jong confirms the positive impact of advertising on sales and indeed, provides a list of several studies on the subject for further reading (Luo and de Jong, 2012).

In other words, to grow, brands need to focus on a long-term brand strategy and invest in marketing programmes and advertising campaigns.

With Digital Evolution, Mass Marketing Is Dying

I've talked about how the digital revolution has made it much easier to target heavy, loyal users based on their online behaviour but—though this approach is easy—it is the wrong pursuit. Brands cannot ignore light and very light users. However, brands should take advantage of the digital revolution by using digital media platforms to reach all consumers, not just the heavy users.

Another effect of the digital explosion has been a misplaced emphasis on e-commerce. While I strongly believe in e-commerce and would encourage brands to explore this space, I wouldn't recommend it at the expense of marketing. E-commerce can help your brand's physical availability, and it should, therefore, be pursued as part of your brand's distribution strategy—but not by sacrificing your marketing efforts aimed at enhancing your brand's mental availability.

SUMMARY

- People are NOT rational. As consumers they DON'T spend time thinking about and evaluating brands carefully and they DON'T believe brands are different from each other.
- Brand growth DOESN'T come from getting heavy and loyal consumers to use more. Light and very light users (who buy the brand infrequently) matter. And retention (of existing customers) is NOT cheaper than acquisition.
- Brand growth CANNOT come by increasing usage (buying frequency). A smaller brand CANNOT have higher usage than the market leader.
- Long-term growth is NOT generated by a series of discrete short-term activities. Retail brands DON'T need monthly promotions to bring consumers in and lift sales. Temporary price-discount promotions DON'T attract non-users who subsequently buy and generate incremental long-term sales.
- With the digital evolution, mass marketing is NOT dying. Focusing more on e-commerce and less on marketing is NOT key to brand growth.

Chapter 3
Mental Availability and Insights: The Nuts and Bolts of Brand Growth

'It is not necessary to change. Survival is not mandatory.'
—W. Edwards Deming

As we've now discovered, consumers don't think long and deep about brand choices. Once a need for a category of products arises ('we're running out of detergent'), they will buy a brand they remember (mental availability), provided it's easy to find (physical availability). The decision of buying one brand over the other is made pretty much on auto-pilot.

Assuming that you have a sales and distribution strategy to ensure physical availability (or, if you don't, that you will seek guidance elsewhere), let me dive into the topic of this chapter (and, indeed, the bulk of the book): building the mental availability of your brand.

There is clear evidence linking the size of a brand to its mental availability. For example, in India's mobile phone market, there is a strong correlation between the market share of a brand and its mental availability (measured as the percentage of total category entry point associations [more later] that a brand enjoys)—Samsung, the market leader with over 35 per cent market share, has the highest mental share (close to 25 per cent), while smaller brands like LG,

Lava, and Karbonn, with less than 10 per cent market share, also have less than 10 per cent mental share (Romaniuk, 2016).

Therefore, to grow market share, a brand needs to grow its mental share—and it can do this by building its mental availability.

Building mental availability starts by making your brand easy to remember through its physical assets (Romaniuk, 2016)—for example, the logo (Nike's swoosh), distinct colours (canary yellow for a Post-it note), sound bites (Airtel's musical sign off on its radio and television spots), mascot (Ronald McDonald for McDonald's), and so on. Using quantitative consumer research to identify which assets are best associated with your brand, you should focus on building these over time. This is the green fees of developing brand identity.

Once you have designed and implemented the appropriate physical assets for your brand, your brand strategy and communication should play a big role in constantly augmenting your brand's mental availability. Recognizing that brand decisions are made at an emotional and intuitive level, and not by careful reasoning, your brand needs to make a subtle emotional connection with consumers—a connection that is relevant to the category. Researcher Jenni Romaniuk calls this 'category entry points' and uses a series of questions as a framework—why, when, where, with whom, with what—that act as cues for the consumer to think about the category.

Finding and getting behind the right consumer insight is a powerful way to make an emotional connection with consumers. To set us off on this path, let me relate a story that I heard early on in my career.

A creative director was taking a walk through New York's Central Park during his lunch break when he came upon a poor, blind man with a sign around his neck that read, 'Please help me. I am blind', and a mug in his hand for people to drop money into. Being a true-blue advertising man, the creative director was more generous with his ideas than with his money. He took his pen, wrote something on the man's sign, and continued on his path for lunch.

When he came back an hour later, he stopped in front of the man again.

'How's it going?' he asked.

'Great!' replied the blind man. 'Things were going okay till an hour ago. But then someone wrote something on my sign and since then I've had a lot more people drop money in my mug.'

The creative director was pleased. 'It was I who wrote that,' he said. 'Your sign now reads, "Please help me. It's springtime and I am blind."'

What was it about the new sign that triggered more generosity in people? I submit that it is the consumer *insight*: people are more sympathetic to a fellow human's disability (and therefore liable to help) if they can better appreciate the context of what the person is missing. Realizing that someone is not able to enjoy the season of spring—which is strongly associated with colour, beauty, and joy—evokes sympathy.

Now, you may argue that this was not an example of building mental availability. After all, people see the sign and make an immediate decision to donate (or not). True, but it triggers an emotional connection that will stay in their memory for a long time to come. In other words, if a week later, they see another blind man with no sign around his neck, chances are they will still associate his plight with missing spring and be more inclined to donate some money. In fact, the memory of someone not being able to see the world in all its glory will stick long after the drift of the season—even when winter falls! That is how crucial a good consumer insight is to building mental availability. And the association does not trigger a rational, reasoned thought process; rather, it generates a quick, unconscious, emotional response that leads to decisive action.

In other words, a powerful insight, communicated well (through good advertising), covertly enters a consumer's memory and triggers purchase (or donation) at the right time. It does this by being interesting, emotionally appealing and likeable because, as researcher Byron Sharp puts it, 'Persuasive arguments are more powerful if they include explicit emotional appeal'. He argues that faced with two statements to advertise Goodyear tyres—A. Goodyear tyres grip the road and reduce your stopping distance; B. Today your child's life may depend on your stopping ability, and

Goodyear tyres reduce your stopping distance and keep your loved ones safe—the second has wider appeal (Sharp, 2010). I submit that this is because it leverages a strong consumer insight relevant to the category (of driving): 'When driving, my child's life is in my hands.'

Standing Out in a Sea of Sameness

Knowing that consumers don't really differentiate between brands and understanding the way they make brand decisions—quickly, intuitively, and emotionally—can help us see why a wholly rational appeal ('10 per cent longer life', 'better cleaning') can fall on deaf ears. An exception to this is when an innovation is being introduced for the first time—for example, when the first digital camera replaced the old camera-with-film or when split air conditioners replaced the noisy fixed ones. At that time, the functional benefit of the innovation is interesting news and will generate sales. But soon (very soon nowadays) competition enters the game, submerging every brand in a sea of sameness.

Most brands don't realize this and keep emphasizing their features (which are similar to other brands). Take the detergents category, for example. I think it is safe to assume that all consumers know that detergents clean clothes. Yet every brand of detergent tells us this. In different ways—and often in very similar ways—they promise us pearly white clothes; stain-free clothes that are a beauty to behold; bright clothes that shine in the dark; and clothes so clean they help our children become class monitors and our spouses CEOs.

In this monotony of homogeneity, suddenly there comes along a detergent that, instead of celebrating clean and white clothes, says, 'Dirt is good.' The brand is Omo, one of Unilever's many successful brands, and the rationale behind their positioning is the consumer insight: 'Getting dirty is good for children to develop.'[3]

---

3 You can watch Omo's commercial on YouTube, at <https://www.youtube.com/watch?v=VZnsrFkwWf4>, accessed on 21 November 2016.

Omo doesn't promise whiter clothes or stain removal—people will rate Omo the same as other brands on these attributes anyway (and presumably Unilever understands this). Instead it has carved out a distinctive *link* to the consumer's memory in an area very relevant to the category. Recognizing the power of this insight, Unilever uses it on its biggest detergent brand in each country, be it Omo in the UK, or Surf in India, or Rinso or Breeze in other markets. Following the 'dirt is good' campaign, Unilever's detergent brand (Omo, Surf, Rinso or Breeze, depending on the country) grew sales tenfold in Asia, becoming the number one brand in most Asian countries, with a market share as high as 70 per cent in some regions (Gosling and Jathanna, 2012).

While admiring Omo's insight, I want to spend another minute on it. Getting dirty is a part of a bigger idea. Being spontaneous, exploring the world, having fun, and just being a kid—*all* of this helps a child grow into a happy, whole adult. So, is 'getting dirty is good for kids to develop' a *narrow* definition of the insight? Yes, if you look at it as a pure human revelation. But if you consider *detergents*, sticking to 'children getting dirty' provides the right link to the category. Go beyond that and you lose the connection.

As we've seen, an insight can be powerful—and Part Two of this book will take us through the simple, step-by-step processes guiding the creation of such insights.

Insights and Brilliant Advertising

A meaningful insight, relevant to the consumer in the category, can help shape a brand's strategy and its advertising. Unfortunately many business leaders today dismiss creativity and traditional advertising as relics of yesterday. They're obsessed with 'digital engagement' and getting their brands into social media. In 2010, Pepsi abandoned the traditional approach of heavy media investment in a creative campaign during the Super Bowl. Instead the company developed a social media campaign called 'Pepsi Refresh Project'. They asked consumers to propose ideas that would benefit society and promised to fund the best ones. The project hit all the success measures of a social media campaign—it generated millions of likes on Facebook and generated thousands of new Facebook followers. But it didn't help Pepsi sell more of its cola drink (Leslie, 2015).

As author Ian Leslie points out, such digital engagement is 'largely pointless'. He writes:

> Light buyers aren't fans of your brand. They don't think of it as special or even unique [. . .] they almost certainly don't follow your brand on Twitter or visit its Facebook page [. . .] they can think of a thousand things they'd rather do than share a "digital experience".

He argues that engaging light buyers requires brands to 'sneak up to them' with content 'in bite-sized chunks' that requires 'negligible mental effort to process' and is 'capable of moving and delighting' (Leslie, 2015).

Developing such advertising—likeable, relevant, and visually arresting—is a *craft* that you can learn. And in Part 3 of this book, I will spend time on CRAFT, a neat acronym that captures the key traits you need.

Conviction: It starts with a strong belief in the power of marketing and creative to propel business and brand growth. With 'Conviction', you will see how brilliant creative campaigns can fuel growth, and you'll hopefully begin to believe in their power.

Resources: You need the right people, with the right skills, to develop great creative campaigns. Clients get the advertising they deserve and in the end it's *your* leadership, passion, and belief that can get you brilliant creative.

Approach: A disciplined approach is the cornerstone for success in sports, in arts, in life . . . and while developing great creative. 'Approach' revolves around the principles of a good process and how you can develop one that is clear, efficient, and practical for your brand.

Foundation: The backbone of brilliant creative is the consumer insight, but how do you bring the insight to life with a creative brief? And once the advertising agency responds to the creative brief with a creative idea, how do you evaluate it and give them feedback that results in brilliant work? 'Foundation' answers this.

Teamwork: Finally, while conviction, resources, approach, and foundation are all important, you need a great relationship with your advertising agency. The key elements of a strong win-win client-agency partnership are covered under 'Teamwork'.

CRAFT is not new; it is just a new way of stating old tenets of developing advertising. Part 3 provides examples of various brands that have followed the principles of CRAFT and, as a result, have developed great creative campaigns—campaigns that have stuck in consumers' minds and, subtly, increased the brands' 'mental availability'. By following what you read in this book, your brand can do it, too, and do it *consistently*.

SUMMARY

- To increase a brand's mental availability, it's important to identify the right physical assets (logo, colours, and so on) through quantitative consumer research, and then focus on building these assets.
- While a new-to-the-world innovation can catch a consumer's interest through its functional benefit, an established brand in a competitive, me-too category needs to rely on making a subtle emotional connection to grow mental availability. Finding the right consumer insight that provides a link to the category is a powerful way to make that emotional connection. The right insight helped Goodyear tyres make a more memorable appeal to consumers and Omo/Surf create a mental association with consumers in the detergent category.
- The insight should shape brand strategy and dictate its advertising campaign. Developing brilliant advertising requires CRAFT: conviction, resources, approach, foundation, and teamwork.

PART TWO

The Insight to Connecting with Consumers

Chapter 4
Deconstructing Insights: The Power of a Human Revelation

'Data, data everywhere, but not a thought to think.'
—John Allen Paulos

We're inundated with data today, and it keeps coming. For perspective, 'more data has been created in the past two years than in the entire previous history of the human race,' writes Bernard Marr in an article for *Forbes* (Marr, 2015). He estimates that by 2020, we will have 44 zettabytes of data (one zettabyte = one trillion gigabytes). That's a lot of data!

This explosion of data is witnessed, most of all, in companies, which have business data, financial data, customer data, shopper data, competitor data, market research data, big data, small data, and medium data. Take McDonald's, for example. It has access to data from more than 35,000 restaurants, covering each transaction made by each customer. It has a track record of daily, weekly, and monthly sales going back decades—analyzed for trends after adjusting for seasonality. The company also regularly gathers consumer data on usage and attitude towards the McDonald's brand and its competitors, and studies this rigorously. It hires third-party analytics to evaluate—by product, by daypart, and by type of restaurant—the impact of pricing on sales, which is then used to guide pricing decisions. In addition to the reams of internal data on finance, real estate, suppliers, and employees,

McDonald's also accesses external data on the economy, consumer eating behaviour, trends in the food service industry, and so on.

Other companies are no different. Businesses today are groaning under the weight of all this data and their leaders are often unsure about what to do. 'Too much data!' senior leaders say. 'We need more insights on businesses to replace all this data.'

And this provides an impetus to an organization to go ahead and do just that—replace data with insights, *literally*! So the list now reads: business insights, financial insights, customer insights, shopper insights, competitor insights, market research insights, big insights, small insights, and medium insights. For example, data showing that 'people are spending less annually after the financial crisis' is now called a 'shopper *insight*'. While there's no disputing the truth of the statement, it offers no insight. Several companies, to acclimatize themselves to the pursuit of 'insights', have started renaming their analysis and research areas—so, we have departments called business insights, consumer insights, and so on.

Let's face it: this change in nomenclature only creates an illusion of a focus on insights. It's far more pertinent for company executives to understand what the word truly means—and how *real* consumer insights can help a brand make an emotional connection with consumers at the entry point to the category and therefore elevate the brand in their memory (or increase mental availability).

What are Insights?

Before delving deeper into what consumer insight is, let's look at how dictionaries define the word 'insight'. The Merriam-Webster dictionary states that an insight is 'the power or act of seeing into a situation: penetration' or 'the act or result of apprehending the inner nature of things or of seeing intuitively.' As for Dictionary.com, it states that an insight is 'an instance of apprehending the true nature of a thing, especially through intuitive understanding: e.g. an insight into 18th century life' or a 'penetrating mental vision or discernment; faculty of seeing into inner character or underlying truth.'

There is an aspect of 'hidden truth' in these definitions. Many organizations and ad agencies employ their own definitions to explain insights. For the purpose of this book, I'm going to use a very specific definition: *an insight is an emotional human revelation relevant to the category that is leveraged to build a brand.*

Let me explain why I like this definition (apart from the fact that I coined it), by highlighting three of its deliberate components.

First, an insight is *an emotional human revelation.* In other words, it discloses something—the 'hidden truth' in the dictionary definitions, or something obscure waiting to be unveiled. The response to a good insight is not so much, 'Yes, of course, I always knew that (yawn)', but 'Yes! I didn't think of it quite like that, but it's so true!'

Take the statement, 'On a clear day, people can see the blue sky.' Is that a true human statement? Undoubtedly. But it's also obvious, mundane, and uninteresting. There is no human *revelation* in it. But if you say, 'People's moods lift when the clouds clear and they see a blue sky,' you enter the space of hidden truths. On hearing that, someone may react, 'Yes! That's a nice way of putting it—I agree!' Another way of describing this human revelation is that it is retrospectively obvious.

Second, an insight should be *relevant to the category.* In other words, while many things may resonate with people at an emotional level, a brand needs an insight that is relevant to the category in which it's competing. This is critical if the brand is to be remembered (or if it is to increase its mental availability). Take the statement you just read: 'People's moods lift when the clouds clear and they see a blue sky.' If you're responsible for the tourism industry in, say, Bali, this could be a relevant insight to promote a sun-drenched beach resort. But if you're responsible for a shampoo brand, this insight is of little value.

I use the word 'category', as opposed to 'brand' deliberately. Some ad agencies define an insight as 'the point where a truth of the consumer's life meets a truth of the brand, creating or cementing a bond between them.' This may sound terrific to the brand manager, but the cold, cruel fact is that consumers don't care much for 'a truth about the brand'. In fact, as we've discussed, most people, whether heavy or light users, are not even exclusive consumers of a specific brand! As Professor Andrew Ehrenberg says, 'Your customers are customers of other brands who occasionally buy you' (Sharp, 2010), and Ian Leslie adds that users 'aren't fans of your brand. They don't think of it as special or even unique' (Leslie, 2015).

But even light users are interested in the category. They may not care deeply about Sunsilk or Pantene individually—and may buy one brand this month and the other the next—but they care about washing their hair. And therein lies the opportunity—looking for an insight related to haircare. So, a shampoo brand might tap into the insight, 'People believe that a bad hair day can turn into a bad day' and position itself on the lines of 'hair confidence to face the day.'

When consumers hear an example of this kind, they often object, 'But that's a generic insight—any brand can use it!' Yes, any brand can use a good insight. In fact, the better the insight or the more it is an emotional human revelation related to the category, the more relevant it is to *any* brand in that category. But that's not bad news, because the spoils will go to the brand that first leverages the insight, provided it does so well. Consumers will link the idea behind the insight ('Hair confidence to face the day' in our example) with this brand. Knowing this, other brands will not follow for fear of confusing its consumers, or, worse, actually promoting the first brand!

That brings us to the third, and the most important, part of our definition: insights must be *leveraged to build a brand*. This means three things. First, the brand should bring the insight to life across its business plans—not just through its advertising, but also through its packaging design, website, sponsorship, and so on. Second, advertising should bring the insight to life brilliantly. And third, the brand should put its money where its insight is. In other words, it should invest confidently and boldly in marketing the insight.

Sometimes a brand may be peculiarly suited to leverage an insight, as you will see in the McDonald's example shortly. But you need not pursue such special, exclusive insights because, I repeat, by leveraging *any* good insight well, you reap long-term business growth from it.

When all three components of the insight are right, the brand can make that subtle, but powerful, emotional connection that elevates it in a consumer's memory.

Case Studies

There are several examples of insights that meet all three criteria. I'd like to talk about two here: McDonald's, a brand I've had experience with, and Dove, a brand that discovered a powerful insight over 15 years ago and used it to shape its entire brand strategy.

McDonald's

'First Day'[4] is a simple TV ad that shows a man on his first day of work. He is introduced to colleagues, exposed to company systems and habits ('We don't normally use more than one towel, Andy') and is taken on a tour of the building. After a few hours, he is overwhelmed. Sitting alone in a room at lunch time, bewildered by the new information, he suddenly pushes back his chair and strides purposefully out of the office building. He walks into a nearby McDonald's, orders a Big Mac meal, takes it to a table, and playfully relaxes over his lunch.

It's a charming advertisement based on a simple, but powerful, insight: 'In times of stress, we seek comfort in the familiar.' Now you may word it differently, and that's fine. It's not important that we articulate an insight in any particular way or agree on the exact set of words—after all, the consumer never actually reads these words. (In fact, I advise the team working on insights to play around with phrases and stop when they arrive at a reasonable statement, as long as everyone agrees that it captures the idea's essence.)

---

4 You can watch the McDonald's commercial on YouTube, at <https://www.youtube.com/watch?v=Qoav_fOFgb8>, accessed on 6 December 2016.

Now what makes the message of 'First Day' a brilliant insight for a McDonald's campaign?

- First, it's a strong *human revelation*. When we're in strange or stressful situations, we like to anchor ourselves in something we know. It brings solace. When exposed to this insight, people will likely say to themselves, 'That's so true! I felt that way when I was in Cambodia!'

- Second, the insight is very *relevant to the category*—eating familiar food is one of life's most relaxing experiences. We don't call it 'comfort food' for nothing!

- And finally, the insight can be effectively *leveraged by the brand*. In fact, McDonald's—as the world's most ubiquitous and familiar restaurant brand serving over 65 million people a day—is perfectly placed to take advantage of this insight, compared to a smaller restaurant chain.

Dove

The second case in point is Dove. In fact, this example from Unilever is such a rich source of learning on insights that I will use it across the book. In the early 2000s (Deighton, 2007), Dove discovered an insight that has shaped the brand's strategy and creative campaigns ever since: 'Many women don't consider themselves beautiful because beauty brands—and society—have ingrained in them a false definition of beauty.' (These are my words but again, what matters is the essence.)

Let's examine Dove's insight against the three parts of our definition:

- The insight is a great *human revelation*—women can readily empathize with the notion that their perception of beauty is distorted because of what brands have taught them.

- The insight is obviously *relevant to the* beauty *category*.

- And finally, the insight can be (and has been) *leveraged* by the brand. With no history of promoting stereotypical notions of beauty—previous Dove advertising campaigns had focused on the soap being 'gentle on skin'—Dove was perfectly poised to break with convention. On the other hand, existing brands like Lux (also under Unilever)—known to use glamorous film actresses to promote beauty—can hardly switch track now. In fact, you may argue that Lux has contributed to making Dove's insight so strong! Besides, later, you will see how Unilever used this simple but powerful insight to shape Dove's entire brand strategy, marketing plan, and advertising approach ('Campaign for Real Beauty').

SUMMARY

- Finding the right insight—an emotional human revelation relevant to the category that your brand can leverage—is the first big step towards building mental availability, which is key to brand growth.
- McDonald's and Dove are two brands that have recognized and exploited the power of insights.

Chapter 5
Do Insights Matter in Today's Digital World? The New Conundrum

'The internet is becoming the town square for the global village of tomorrow.'
—Bill Gates

Most marketing people would agree that insights played an important role in marketing when brands advertised on traditional media like television, radio, and print. But they ask: do insights really matter in an era when consumers are so busy and digitally engaged all the time? The answer is yes. In fact, they matter even more today!

Insights and the ESCAPE-ing Consumer

Let's first step back and understand what role insights played in the pre-digital age, in the 1980s and 1990s—the heyday of mass marketing and of big advertising budgets.

A lot of thought was put into developing the media plan. A brand targeting young working adults, for example, would observe a typical day in these people's lives—they wake up and get ready to go to work (eating breakfast hurriedly, while also reading the paper); commute to an office; work there until evening, taking a break only for lunch; and commute home, perhaps stopping to shop on the way. Once home, they eat dinner and then sit down to watch television before hitting the bed. The brand's media plan would be based on this behaviour:

using print ads in newspapers that these consumers could read while getting ready for work; appealing to them on the radio or through outdoor advertising while they were commuting; advertising in-store while they shopped; and finally, saving the most powerful weapon in the arsenal for the end, mesmerizing them with emotional, insightful, and well-produced television campaigns after dinner, during prime time. Figure 5.1 captures this situation pictorially.

Figure 5.1 The Consumer's Day and the Marketer's Job: 20 Years Ago

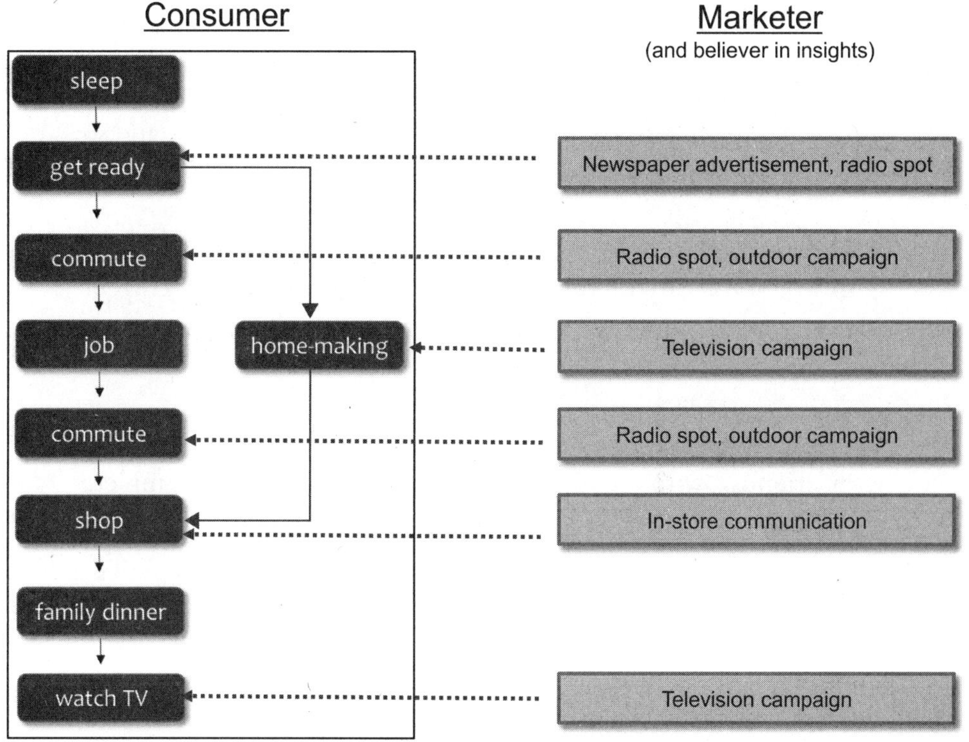

If that was approach in the pre-digital era when insights made all the difference, let us look at *today's* young adults. While they essentially still do the same things as any working adult back then, something intrusive is occupying their entire waking lives—their digital world. Whether they work in an office, school, factory or at home—or even if they don't work at all—consumers today are constantly involved in digital activity.

I believe there are six distinct digital activities that can be neatly captured in the acronym ESCAPE: engaging, shopping, creating, ascertaining, playing, and entertaining.

Engaging: People constantly connect with other people—chat, email, and message via social media—and share things they come across that they like (and dislike) such as news articles, videos, reviews, tweets, and so on.

Shopping: People use the internet for online shopping. Not surprisingly, the e-commerce space is growing every day.

Creating: A small but influential number of people develop content from scratch—like blogs, articles, reviews, videos, podcasts, and so on—and post these on the internet for others to access.

Ascertaining: People use the internet to acquaint themselves with just about anything under the sun—from news and current affairs, to advice and reviews, to novel recipes and new restaurants (and the fastest routes to get there).

Playing: People play all sorts of games on the internet—alone, with friends, with family members, and even with complete strangers.

Entertaining: The internet has become a huge pastime for people; they watch movies and shows, follow sports, and listen to music.

ESCAPE-ing has transformed the behaviour of the typical working adult. Even the very first activity—'wake up and get ready'—has been upended. A 2013 study by Facebook and IDC (International Data Corporation) showed that a whopping 79 per cent of people who own a smartphone in the USA check it as soon as they wake up before doing anything else (Adweek, 2013). They continue to ESCAPE while getting ready—scouring the internet for things of interest, catching online news, listening to their favourite playlist or texting while on the step-machine in the gym or over breakfast. During a long commute, ESCAPE is the dominant activity; almost everyone in the train or bus is face down, staring at a smartphone screen. (In fact, such is the intensity of focus on mobile devices that I often wonder whether anyone would even notice if all buses and trains were to suddenly board up their windows with opaque material!) After dinner, families may be physically together but every member is individually ESCAPE-ing. As Lindsay Rothfeld observes, 'Today, family members sit engrossed in their individual tablets, binge-watching the latest on Netflix, Hulu or Amazon Instant' (Rothfeld, 2014).

Millennials—the generation that reached young adulthood around the year 2000—exemplify this propensity to ESCAPE, and it's fair to say that Gen Z, people born roughly after the mid-1990s and straight into a world of digital devices, have been ESCAPE-ing since infancy. But, while ESCAPE-ing may come as naturally as breathing to these younger generations, in reality everyone is ESCAPE-ing to some degree today.

Coming back then to the question at the beginning of this chapter, surely if we needed insights to connect with the pre-digital consumer who was much less distracted, we need them that much more to connect with highly busy, digitally-engrossed ESCAPE-ing consumers today, who we know are not really, deeply interested in brands. In other words, insights have never been more important!

Insights Can Shape Business Strategy and Brand Positioning

McDonald's became the world's biggest restaurant chain by meeting the need for convenient, affordable, tasty food. But as the brand expanded and began advertising for the first time, it did not emphasize the *functional* benefits of convenience that it offered, rightly concluding that others could easily offer this. Instead, over the years, McDonald's has leveraged powerful insights in its brand strategy ('simple, easy enjoyment') and advertising. For example, it used the insight, 'People need some respite to cope with life' in a long-lasting campaign called 'You deserve a break today', which helped build the brand into the powerhouse that it is. (Over the years McDonald's has leveraged other strong insights, which you will see later in the book.)

Similarly Apple's success is based on building innovative products that meet consumers' needs. In positioning itself, the brand leveraged a simple insight—'People find technology intimidating'—and, in the advertising for its Mac, highlighted the user-friendly nature of the brand.

So if McDonald's and Apple have been built on strong concepts and powerful insights, let's look at Uber, the fresh kid on the block, that has begun the same journey to become a powerful brand.

Uber

At its core Uber addresses the same need for convenience that McDonald's did. But convenience is particularly relevant today. People's lives are not just busy, they are frantically hectic. They manage a tough job in a difficult job market; navigate a hectic social life; stay close to their family; and, don't forget, ESCAPE all the time! Time is the biggest crunch they face and they're constantly looking for ideas and devices that will save them a few minutes and make their lives easier. And the underlying insight here—'Time and convenience are the most valuable currencies for today's digital generation'—is what Uber addresses with its business model.

- Uber offers the most convenient public transport. It's easy to order a vehicle when you need it—press a few buttons and a car shows up at your doorstep with the driver already aware of your destination. When you reach your journey's end, you simply walk out. Your ride is automatically charged to your card. The whole service is about time-saving and convenience.

- Uber also allows you to share the ride with a friend and split the fare with ease—another convenience model. They've now augmented this feature in many markets to allow you to share the ride with a complete stranger through UberPOOL (Ong, Josh, 2014).

- The company is experimenting with adjunct services like food delivery under the name UberFRESH or UberEATS (McGregor, 2014) and a courier service called UberRUSH.

Another insight that Uber addresses is: 'People want more certainty and control over their lives than ever before.' The omniscient internet has given us so much power over our lives that we now want it all the time. (Consider this, for instance: when viewing orchids in a park, we may want to know more about orchids in Africa, how orchids compare with other flowers, where they grow best, and how they're used in Chinese medicine. Without getting up from our bench in the park, and perhaps paying little attention to the actual orchids near us, we seek the answers on Google through our mobile phone. And if we find it interesting enough, we broadcast the information via social media.)

Addressing this desire for *control*, Uber allows you to track your route when you're travelling or track the route your daughter takes at night while you're at home worrying about her safety. It also allows you to rate the driver. Both these features help heighten your sense of control over your life.

Uber's third insight—'Being driven in a private car is a sign of success'—is powerful, and isn't peculiar to today's digital consumer alone; it is age-old. With the selling line—'Everyone's private driver'—Uber acknowledges and addresses this. The company is now experimenting with an extension of this insight, namely that being driven in Lamborghinis and Maseratis is an even stronger sign of success (Liu, 2015).

Figure 5.2 summarizes how the Uber business model addresses the insights I just talked about.

Figure 5.2 Insights (Especially for ESCAPE-ing Consumers) and the Uber Model

Insight	Uber's business model
'Time and convenience are the most valuable currencies for today's generation.'	The most convenient public transport system in terms of ordering, using, and paying.
	Share the ride, share the cost.
	(Experiments) Food delivery, courier service.
'I want control over the things I buy and use.'	You rate the driver; the driver rates you.
	Track the route on the app while you're moving.
'Being driven in a private car is a sign of success.'	'Everyone's private driver.'

Uber was launched in 2009 and began expanding—a city per month—in the USA in 2011. It went international a year later (actually by launching in the place where the founders Garrett Camp and Travis Kalanick had come up with the idea, Paris), and in the few short years since then, has expanded across over a 100 cities (as of April 2014). The company is valued at more than $10 billion (Chokkattu and Crook, 2014). This success can be attributed to Uber addressing its powerful insights about consumers today, just as the success of McDonald's and Apple can be traced back to the insights *they* addressed.

SUMMARY

- With constant access to a digital world, customers today are ESCAPE-ing all the time—engaging, shopping, creating, ascertaining, playing, entertaining—even while pursuing other activities.
- To capture today's consumer's attention and increase the brand's mental availability, insights are particularly important. A relevant insight can influence brand strategy, shape the business model, and impel sales growth, as it did for McDonald's, Apple, and, most recently, Uber.

Chapter 6
Busting Common Myths: A Measured Understanding of Insights

'Belief in myths allows the comfort of opinion without the discomfort of thought.'
—John F. Kennedy

Like the myth that insights don't matter in today's digital world, there are a few other myths that we need to bust.

1. Insights play a role only in television advertising.
2. An insight is nice if you find it, but it's no big deal if you don't.
3. It's the agency's job to find insights.
4. We need to constantly find new insights.
5. An insight reflects a deep understanding of the consumer's psyche.
6. An insight needs to highlight a consumer problem.

Let's take them one by one.

Myth #1: Insights Play a Role Only in Television Advertising

In March 2013, Coca-Cola and its advertising agency Leo Burnett Worldwide performed an experiment called 'Small World Machines' that took advertising by storm—without relying on television.

Instead Coca-Cola relied on a different machine—a pair of them actually—which allowed people to interact across a distance. Essentially, these were hi-tech vending machines with large 3D digital screens. Coca-Cola installed one in Lahore, Pakistan and another in New Delhi, India, each in a crowded mall with a lot of people passing by. Words on the screen beckoned the Indian to 'make a friend in Pakistan (to share a Coca-Cola)'; similar words invited his counterpart in Lahore to participate.

When you walked towards the screen, you could see someone approaching it, through the glass, in the other country. Instructions on the screen then urged you to 'join hands' figuratively with this stranger, to trace a smiley face or the international sign of peace together, to dance, to share a Coke . . . and, in the end, to simply connect as humans do. By doing this, you discovered that the other person—commonly portrayed as the 'bad guy'—was, in fact, much like you. You were then rewarded with a Coca-Cola that you could virtually share with your new friend on the other side.

The activation ran for three days and resulted in more than 10,000 cans of Coca-Cola being consumed on both sides. Most importantly, it generated optimism amongst participants and, through them, in over 3 million others who watched the experiment on YouTube.[5] One participant said, 'It is more about how similar we are, as opposed to how different we are.' A counterpart put it more succinctly: 'Togetherness, humanity, this is what we want. More and more exchange.'

In the words of Andy DiLallo, chief creative officer of Leo Burnett Sydney (Ricki, 2013):

> To be able to take two countries that have been divided and to unite them through the world's most iconic brand, and see the purity of the experience was amazing [. . .] Small World Machines is a real-world example of the power of creativity.

---

5 You can watch the Coca-Cola experiment on YouTube, at <https://www.youtube.com/watch?v=ts_4vOUDImE>, accessed on 7 December 2016.

Why did this activation resonate so strongly with people? Because it was based on a very powerful insight: 'What unites people is stronger than what separates them.'

Polar Beer, a brand of beer sold in just one state in Brazil, conducted another mindboggling experiment in a few bars in Brazil. Calling it 'using technology against technology', they designed a beer cooler that not only kept the beer cool, but also covertly blocked all signals—GSM, Wi-Fi, GPS, 3G, and 4G—from any phone within a five-foot radius. The result: people seated at the table with the beer cooler were forced to interact with their friends without getting distracted by their smartphones. The experiment was widely popular; the video showcasing it was one of the ten most-viewed advertisements on YouTube spontaneous media.[6]

Why did the Polar Beer idea take off? Because it was based on a fundamental insight particularly true of today's consumer: 'Immersed in their digital social connections, people forget about the real human interaction they long for.' That the omnipresent smartphone has upended our real-life social interactions is a significant human revelation, and it is not a surprise that people actually welcomed the forced separation from their devices so they could spend quality time with their friends.

Now, both Coca-Cola and Polar Beer leveraged very strong insights—one forced people to reconsider their deep-rooted prejudices against their neighbours, popularly portrayed as villains; and the other made people rethink their social behaviour. Yet neither brand used a television advertisement to bring the insight to life.

The question then is: could a television advertisement have brought these insights to life as well as the activation programmes? I don't think so. The truth is that insights can be equally (if not more) powerful when conveyed through real-life experiments (that go viral).

---

6 You can watch the Polar Beer experiment on YouTube, at <https://www.youtube.com/watch?v=fN7Fg0LWZsI>, accessed on 7 December 2016.

Myth #2: An Insight is Nice If You Find It, but It's No Big Deal If You Don't

In an earlier chapter, I had described how, in the detergent category, where all brands promise stain-free clothes, the Unilever detergent brand Omo embraced an insight that helped it to stand apart: 'Dirt is good for kids to develop.'

Here's another example: McDonald's French fries. Whether or not you agree that they are the tastiest fries on the planet, you will have to concede that they're the most consumed. McDonald's French fries have the mathematical advantage!

McDonald's has always promoted its fries as being irresistibly tasty. Now, that's a neat benefit, but for that very reason many snacking brands claim to be irresistibly tasty (Pringles and Lay's to name just two).

So, early in its marketing journey, McDonald's discovered a fresh insight to bring 'irresistibly tasty' to life: 'When confronted with something tasty, even honest people are tempted to steal.' That's so true, isn't it? If a stranger seated next to you left a wallet unattended for a few minutes, you wouldn't dream of taking a few currency notes out of it (I hope!). But what if they left behind an opened packet of your favourite chips, or chocolates, or peanuts? The insight is relevant to the entire snacking category and therefore can be used by any snacking brand—and McDonald's seized it for its French fries.

In the 1990s, it came out with a charming advertisement in the USA. In a crowded office elevator, a timid and small-made man clutches on to a box of McDonald's fries; he is surrounded by bigger men, who look at the fries with envy. One of the big guys says, 'You know, if this elevator ride were any longer, you'd have to fight us for those fries!' Everyone laughs; even the diminutive owner of the fries joins in, albeit a little nervously. A few seconds later, the elevator actually comes to a shaky stop mid-journey. Someone says, 'We're stuck!' And as the film closes, we see everyone moving a little closer to the fries . . .[7]

This insight has served McDonald's well over the years, and across the globe. In the early 2000s, it was used in an advertisement in China, where two friends, who grow up sharing everything, suddenly guard their McDonald's fries from one another; and in Korea, where a man surreptitiously tries to pick a solitary fry from a box resting on his sleeping neighbour's chest (and unfortunately gets caught). The latest is less than three years old. It's from the Philippines and features a man in a gym who spies a packet of McDonald's fries on a bench and, after looking around to ensure that nobody is watching, stealthily takes one. Just then, a locker door closes to reveal the owner of the fries—a famous boxer in the country—catching him in the act.

All these advertisements have helped McDonald's successfully sell fries. Consumers relate to the ad protagonists ('That could be me!') and this helps create subtle positive memories of the food item being advertised. So, the next time they're hungry, their recollections can trigger the impulse to eat McDonald's French fries (or if they're in McDonald's, to include fries in their order). As we now know, such decisions happen on auto-pilot, based on a brand's emotional and mental availability. Insightful advertising quietly and imperceptibly enhances the brand's mental availability.

In other words, an insight is not just 'nice if you find it'. As the McDonald's fries example shows, the right insight can generate a brand-differentiating, long-term competitive advantage.

A word of caution here. Since the insight is true to the category, it's important for McDonald's to continue promoting it and investing in it. This will prevent other brands from getting behind the same insight. For example, if KFC were to use an insight promoted by McDonald's for its fries, it would trigger a familiar association in the consumer's mind, who would automatically think of McDonald's.

---

7 You can watch the McDonald's commercial on Advertolog, at <http://www.advertolog.com/mcdonalds/adverts/elevator-337955>, accessed on 10 December 2016.

In other words, KFC's advertising would inadvertently work to promote McDonald's! For this reason, KFC would not pursue this path. (And there is no need to—KFC can find other, equally compelling insights.) But if McDonald's were to abandon this insight, after a few years a different brand could plant its flag on it.

Myth #3: It's the Agency's Job to Find Insights

There are several leaders who do not fully grasp the power of consumer insights. But even among those who do, many don't proactively take charge of insight development, and leave this task to agencies because they believe:

(1) The agency's creative idea sparks the insight.
(2) Creative people are better at articulating insights.

Let's look at both.

It is true that the agency's creative people can come up with ideas that lead to insights. But therein lies the problem. By depending on the creative team for ideas that contains insights, you assume that you will ultimately get the best insight to address your business. Imagine the power of *first* identifying the most relevant insight for your business situation and then unleashing your creative people to find different, imaginative ways to bring it to life!

It's also true that creative people can effectively express their ideas through words. However, as I've already explained, the words describing the insight are not crucial because consumers never actually read the insight statement—they see how it's implemented in the marketing plan and creative execution. What's important is that everyone in the team of marketing and agency people has a common understanding of, and a strong belief in, the insight.

Here's how I recommend you approach the task of developing insights. Start with the business challenge—either an issue to be resolved or an opportunity to be exploited. Once the business challenge is demarcated:

(1) Articulate the challenge: clearly identify the business issue you're trying to solve or the opportunity you're trying to exploit.

(2) Compile all the data relevant to this challenge—internal data like consumer research, business facts, competition, and so on; and external data like consumer trends, economic indicators, and pertinent syndicated research.

(3) Distil the data into useful knowledge ('nuggets of knowledge' is my term for this) by following some interesting and time-tested brainstorming techniques.

(4) Write insights based on the 'nuggets of knowledge'.

(5) Build full-fledged action plans based on the insights.

Teamwork is critical to bring all of this together. While the agency can play a very useful role especially in step 4—that is, writing the insight from the 'nuggets of knowledge'—company executives are best at steps 1, 2, and 3—that is, defining the challenge, collating all relevant information on it, and developing the best 'nuggets of knowledge' for step 4 based on this. And if both company and agency people put their heads together to develop a plan of action for an insight (step 5), the results will be exceptional.

Figure 6.1 captures what I just said pictorially.

Figure 6.1 Developing Insights as a Team

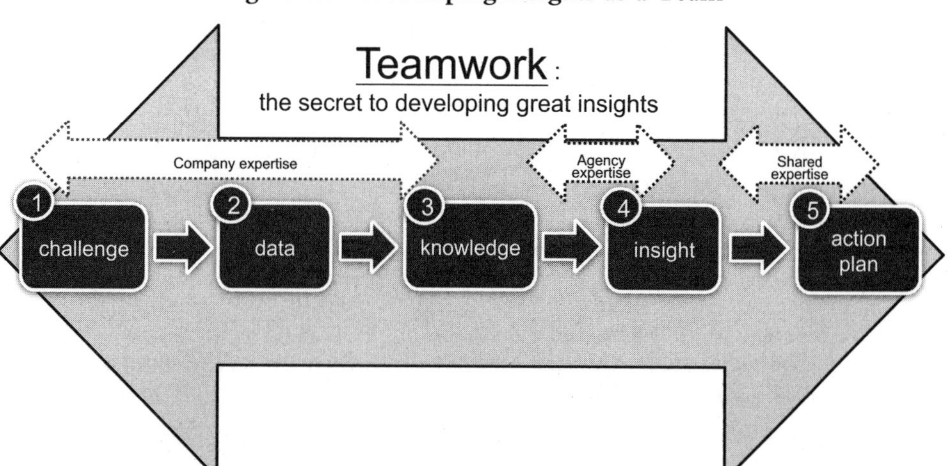

When you follow the process I've described, you will come up with several insights. You should select one or two that best address your business challenge; are intimately linked to your category; can be exploited by your brand; and can stand the test of time. And this process is best done as a client-agency team.

Myth #4: We Need to Constantly Find New Insights

No, we don't, not every time. If the right insight is found—as with Dove and women's perception of beauty—not only can it define brand strategy for years, but it can also travel across continents (as we saw in the McDonald's French fries example).

It's possible that an insight is relevant but cannot cover the scope and compass of a brand. Let's look at the McDonald's 'First Day' ad again, which leveraged the insight that in times of stress we seek comfort in the familiar. Now, that's a very relevant and powerful insight for McDonald's, but the brand cannot rely solely on it. After all, McDonald's is a big brand, not just in terms of its customer base and revenue but also in its appeal; it is a meal, a snack, and a place of refuge; it's convenient, accessible, and inexpensive; it has different offers across the day; it has a drive-through and a delivery service; and it's a playful sanctuary for children, among other things. Therefore, in its brand advertising journey, it must leverage multiple powerful insights (such as 'there's a playful child inside every adult'[8] and 'in a world where they have to constantly live up to others' expectations, people crave an unpretentious environment where they are welcome, no matter who they are or how they dress'[9]). But, though McDonald's may tap into many insights, it does not need to constantly find new ones. It can focus on a few and find different, refreshing ways to communicate them.

8 You can watch an example of 'a playful child in every adult' in this advertisement from McDonald's Australia on YouTube, at <https://www.youtube.com/watch?v=RbCvmhcBFsM>, accessed on 12 December 2016.

9 Here are two examples of McDonald's standing for 'an unpretentious environment where people are welcome, whoever they are', one from the UK via YouTube, at <https://www.youtube.com/watch?v=gpHO1dYIoDY>, and the other from France via YouTube, at <https://www.youtube.com/watch?v=9xGRii6IA1M>, both accessed on 12 December 2016.

Myth #5: An Insight Reflects a Deep Understanding of the Consumer's Psyche

One reason why marketers who understand the power of insights don't spend time pursuing them (or leave the job to an agency) is the enormity of the task confronting them. They think that an insight is a mental breakthrough pertinent to a consumer, and believe that they don't have the necessary skills—a complex understanding of human psychology, perhaps—to develop it.

Well, they're wrong. To develop an insight, all they need is an understanding of the business, the challenges it faces, and the target consumer—all well within the capacity of a cross-functional team in a company's marketing and research departments and the advertising agency. I'd like to cite a couple of examples from a completely different area of study—driving and road accidents.

According to the World Health Organization, about 1.24 million people die from road accidents every year; and another 20 to 50 million sustain non-fatal injuries. And, according to Bob Joop Goos, chairman of the International Organisation for Road Accident Prevention, 'More than 90 per cent of road accidents are caused by human error'(Olarte, 2011). To reduce accidents caused by such 'human error', Mr Goos asserts that we 'have to focus on people in our traffic safety programmes'.

But how is this to be done? By finding insights relevant to driving and accidents.

One insight is linked to the largest contributor to 'human error': driving under the influence of alcohol. In fact, looking at data from the USA alone, between 1975 and 2014, drunk driving led to over 585,000 fatalities, not far behind the 725,000 odd deaths caused by murder (Hansen, 2014).

Despite knowing the risk, what makes people drink and drive? It is conceit. While drinking alcohol actually reduces people's reaction time and dullens their motor senses, it simultaneously fills them with a false sense of confidence that their reaction time and motor senses have been heightened! In other words: 'Under the influence of alcohol, people believe they're superheroes.'

The automobile manufacturer Volkswagen, in a public service campaign, cleverly leveraged this insight. Each ad showed superheroes (Superman, Hulk, Wolverine, and so on) lying dead next to their crashed vehicles. The tagline was: 'Don't let your ego drive you. If you drink don't drive.'[10]

The second insight revolves around another reason for 'human error'—callousness and a lack of regard for human life. The Brazilian agency Heads Propaganda tapped into this and developed a provocative, deliberately exaggerated insight: 'Many people consider driving an entertainment sport, much like hunting.' They then brought the insight to life through a thought-provoking poster advertisement featuring a bicycle handlebar on a wall like a trophy (similar to the heads and torsos of animals that hunters display on their walls), with a tagline that read: 'Hunted in the park' (Min, 2014). The explanation below the picture said: 'Every day, more and more cyclists are being killed in Brazilian streets and roads. Let's respect the cyclists. Let's stop hunting.'[11] By exaggerating the villainy of the motorist, the insight makes the average driver think about—and reconsider—his recklessness.

I'm going to list the insights in these two examples and follow this up with the three examples I shared earlier:

- Under the influence of alcohol, people believe they're superheroes (Volkswagen).

- Many people consider driving an entertainment sport, much like hunting (Heads Propaganda).

---

10 You can view a Volkswagon advertisement at <http://designtaxi.com/news/368189/Volkswagen-Ads-Feature-Drunk-Superheroes-Behind-The-Wheel/>, accessed on 24 February 2017.

11 You can view a Heads Propaganda advertisement at <https://adsoftheworld.com/media/print/respeite_um_carro_a_menos_hunted_in_the_park>, accessed on 24 February 2017.

- Many women don't consider themselves beautiful because beauty brands—and society—have ingrained in them false definitions of beauty (Dove).
- Dirt is good for kids to develop (Omo detergent).
- When confronted with something tasty, even honest people are tempted to steal (McDonald's French fries).

These aren't exactly deep explorations of the human psyche; rather they are simple human revelations that prompt a nod and a silent 'Ah, that's so true' from those exposed to them. In essence, these are five simple statements that capture what people think or do.

So, don't be in awe of the word 'insights'. You, along with your marketing team and agency, can develop and leverage them in your business plans and advertising. And when you do, you will reap the rewards of brand growth!

Myth #6: An Insight Needs to Highlight a Consumer Problem

This is a strange perception held by some people. Granted, some insights do highlight a problem. Among the ones we just reviewed, for example, the ads on road accidents do focus on an area of general concern. The Dove insight does, too. But there's no reason to assume that every insight needs to be based on a consumer issue. Insights can be joyful and fun, and still have a meaningful, emotional impact.

To get the creative juices flowing, you may like to conjure up some 'happy' insights. Here are a few that will help trigger your imagination.

- **A familiar smell can evoke joyous memories of childhood.** Who has not been reminded of a pleasant, almost forgotten childhood event by the scent of something? If your brand has been around for a while—ever since your current adult target audience was much younger—and is associated with a specific fragrance, isn't 'a familiar smell evokes joyous memories of childhood' a great insight to leverage? Equally, if your brand is young, but carries scents entwined with childhood adventures, the insight remains relevant. Paper Boat, an Indian beverage brand, which packages 'favourite old flavours in a new avatar', would agree![12]

- **When you're in love, everything looks wonderful.** Here's another happy insight especially relevant to companies in the business of romance—those affiliated with engagement rings, greeting cards, dining . . . the list can be quite long. Indeed, if you're in love, you may ask, 'What is not romantic?'

- **Children grow into happy adults when they see that their parents are happy.** If you're working in the area of children's wellbeing—with UNICEF, for instance—is this not a powerful and happy insight to use? One could also flip the insight, so it is sad but powerful: 'Children become destructive when their parents behave destructively.' In fact, the Australian agency NAPCAN (National Association for the Prevention of Child Abuse and Neglect) leveraged this insight in a powerful campaign called 'Children see. Children do' (Macleod, 2006).[13]

- **For many people, a dog is more a child than a pet.** If you have a pet, or know someone who does, you may nod in agreement. It's a powerful insight, perfect for a company in the business of grooming pets, and it's a thoroughly joyous one.

I hope this chapter has left you with a smile and renewed faith in the power of consumer insights.

---

12 You can watch one of Paper Boat's advertisements on YouTube, at <https://www.youtube.com/watch?v=dzAdsXpKun4>, accessed on 12 December 2016.
13 You can watch the NAPCAN campaign on YouTube, at <https://www.youtube.com/watch?v=jOrGsB4qG_w>, accessed on 12 December 2016.

SUMMARY

- Insights are not only important for television advertising but also for all creative campaigns, including–if not especially–digital ones.
- Insights are a big deal. The right insight can shape a differentiating, long-term brand strategy.
- When a company's marketing team works with an agency, such teamwork can produce truly powerful, long-term insights.
- We don't need to constantly find new insights. Big brands have built themselves by staying true to one insight for many years.
- An insight does not necessarily reflect a deep understanding of the consumer psyche. It could be a simple observation of human behaviour.
- An insight need not highlight a consumer problem. It can be a joyful, life-affirming statement!

Chapter 7
Building Knowledge: The Foundation for Insights

'Practice doesn't make perfect. Practice reduces the imperfection.'
—*Toba Beta*

Sometimes one may stumble upon a great insight on a brand during the creative process. But relying on luck is hardly a sound business strategy. Instead, one could follow a simple but rigorous process—by collaborating with the right people—to discover strong insights with certainty, just like Dove did.

Dove is an excellent example of an insight leveraged by teamwork and sheer conviction. Many reports and case studies dwell on this—among them, the Harvard Business School case study by John Deighton (Deighton, 2007), from which I have gleaned the following facts.

In the year 2000, Unilever embarked upon an ambitious plan for Dove—to upgrade it from a soap to a beauty brand. In company lingo, the organization wished to transform Dove into a 'masterbrand'. Why was this ambitious? Because for the previous half-century or so, Dove's campaign, created by Unilever's ad agency Ogilvy & Mather, had focused on the soap's very functional benefit: 'Dove doesn't dry your skin because it is one-quarter cleansing cream'. Over the years, that slogan had been tweaked a little—for example, 'cleansing cream' became 'moisturizing cream'—but the essence of the message remained unchanged.

To transform Dove, Unilever relied on consumer research on women and their perception of beauty. It soon discovered that most women had a poor opinion of their own attractiveness because they believed they were not 'young, white, blonde, and thin' enough. To understand this further Unilever engaged two experts—Nancy Etcoff, a psychologist and faculty member of Harvard Medical School, and author of the book *Survival of the Prettiest*; and Susie Orbach, a psychotherapist from London, who had treated, among others, Princess Diana, and authored *Fat Is a Feminist Issue*. The experts came up with hypotheses that Unilever then tested on consumers (with surveys reaching over 3,000 women in 10 countries). Here were some of the key findings from the report that followed:

- Very few women had a high opinion of their own beauty. Only 2 per cent described the way they look as 'beautiful'; only 1 per cent described themselves as either 'sophisticated', 'sexy' or 'stunning'; less than 10 per cent felt they were 'pretty', 'cute', 'good-looking', 'feminine' or 'attractive'. In fact, the highest response was for 'natural' (at 31 per cent) and 'average' (at 25 per cent).

- Many women (68 per cent in Brazil, 28 per cent in Canada) felt that beautiful women had greater opportunities in life; many also felt that 'physically attractive women are more valued by men' (71 per cent in France, 40 per cent in the Netherlands).

- A large number of women (91 per cent in Brazil, 75 per cent in the UK, 41 per cent in Japan) wished that 'the media did a better job of portraying women of diverse physical attractiveness—age, shape and size'.

The people at Dove made a bold move—they decided to challenge stereotypes by developing a powerful insight. How did they achieve this end? By precisely following the five steps that I briefly covered in the previous chapter (refer to Figure 6.1).

(1) They *articulated the business challenge*—transforming Dove from a mere soap to a beauty brand.

(2) They *compiled all the data relevant to this challenge* by studying women's perception of beauty.

(3) They *distilled the data into useful knowledge* by asking experts to provide some hypotheses, which they then researched further, leading to the definitive conclusion that women had poor self-esteem in matters concerning their own attractiveness.

(4) They then *wrote the insight* —'Women don't consider themselves beautiful because of socially imposed beauty yardsticks'—based on this knowledge.

(5) Finally, they *created Dove's entire brand strategy and marketing plan* based on this insight.

This approach, especially steps 3 (building knowledge) and 4 (writing insights), depends on good brainstorming techniques. The intention is to first *open the mind* to possibilities (divergence) and then *bring it back* to focus on a powerful idea (convergence). Nathan Proudlove expresses this elegantly in his technical treatise on brainstorming *Search Widely, Choose Wisely*: 'Divergence is supported through various creativity techniques such as brainstorming and lateral thinking, convergence through insight processes' (Proudlove, 1998).

Before getting into each step, it will be useful to review four brainstorming principles, adapted from an excellent compilation on this topic (Saunders, 1999).

Four Brainstorming Principles

1. **Invite the right people to contribute.** It is important that the insight development exercise is done by people who 'get it'.

Ensure the participation of key members of the company working on the brand as well as 'superstars' known for their knowledge of the consumer or their contribution to ideas (even if they're working on another brand at that moment). From the agency include the key planners, client servicing, and creative people. Don't fill the room with numbers—quality trumps quantity in this case (as it does in most cases!). I suggest you target no less than 10 people and no more than 20.

2. **Include the group while defining the problem.** Go through the business challenge with the group—help them understand it and, if required, elaborate its dimensions. It's important for everyone to be on the same page before you brainstorm.

3. **Don't allow good ideas to be discounted.** Brainstorming should be done without constraints. One way to do this, according to Jack Ricchiuto, author of *Collaborative Creativity*, is by *not* thinking about whether the idea is practical and can be implemented.

4. **Give shyer participants anonymity.** Many quiet people may have very good ideas but are too self-conscious to speak up. From time to time allow them to write down ideas and share them in a non-threatening manner. I advocate the use of Post-it notes to capture thoughts individually and paste these on a wall. Apart from giving everyone, including the quiet ones, an equal chance to contribute, Post-it notes allow you to combine ideas by moving them around and playing with them on the board.

Let us now examine each of the five steps of the process to develop insights. I will cover steps 1 to 3 in this chapter, step 4 in Chapters 8 and 9, and step 5 in Chapter 10. And to illustrate all the steps I will use the example of a hypothetical restaurant company named 'Real Foods' introducing a delivery service.

Steps 1 and 2: Articulating the Challenge and Compiling Relevant Data

The first two tasks involve clearly enunciating the business challenge and gathering all the pertinent data.

For Real Foods, let me articulate the business challenge: to launch a delivery service so people can order and consume the restaurant's food in the convenience of their home (or elsewhere).

To collect all the data relevant to this challenge, Real Foods will need to get:

(A) Their sales by time of day, and by dine-in versus takeaway versus drive-through

(B) How consumers rate food delivery services (this will give us a feel for 'consumption outside the restaurant')

(C) The competition—who else is providing food delivery services in the surrounding areas, how well they're doing, and why

(D) Trends in food and other delivery services, and their reasons for growth

(E) Operations of delivery—what Real Foods is good at and what needs improvement, how they fare compared to other delivery providers, and so on

Step 3: Distilling the Data into Useful Knowledge

The aim of this step is to build useful statements—or 'nuggets of knowledge'—from all the data collected. As mentioned in the previous chapter, I view 'developing knowledge' as an area of company expertise and 'writing insights' as an area of agency expertise because of the peculiar strengths they bring to the table. (And I view 'developing the insight action plan' as shared expertise because both parties can contribute equally in this step.) However, to get the best out of this process, it's important for all the steps to be done by both the marketing and agency teams.

Figure 7.1 Steps Within Step 3: Organizing Knowledge

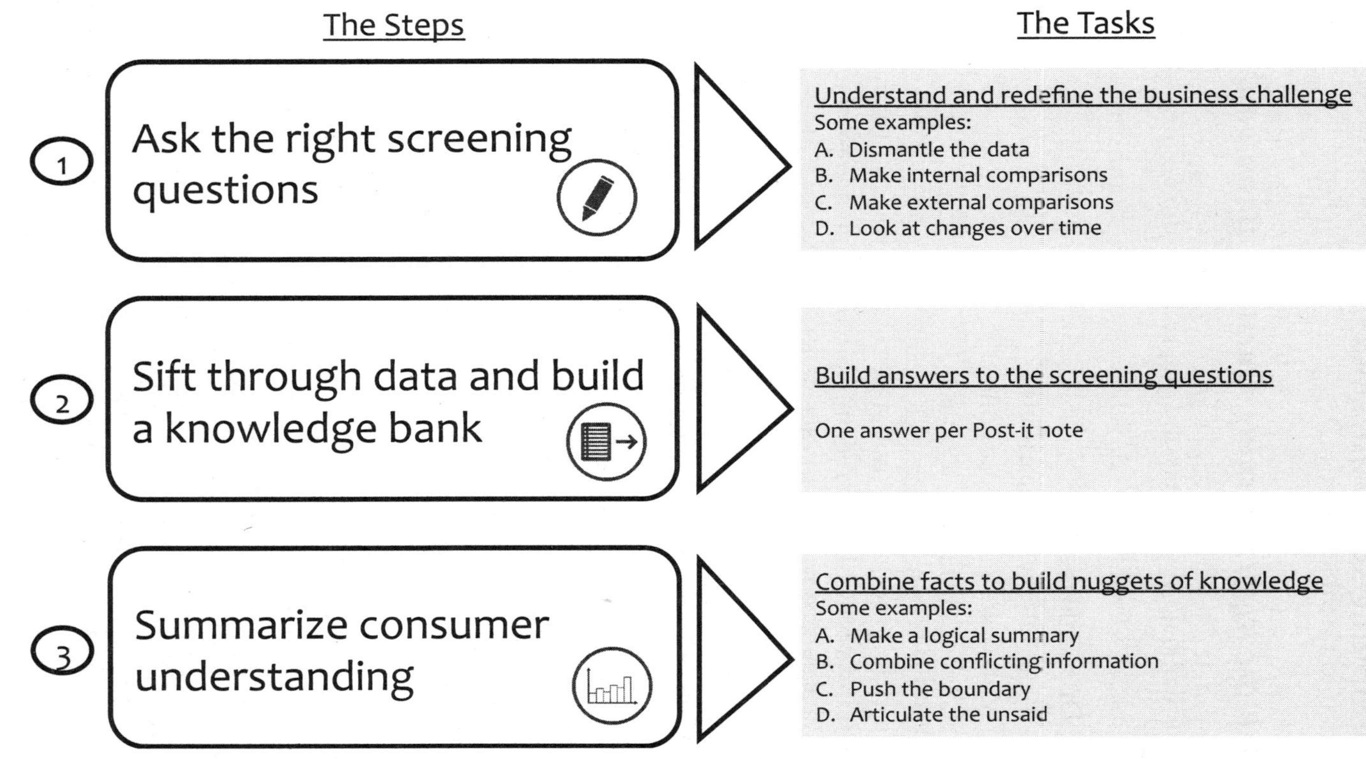
The Steps
The Tasks
1
Ask the right screening questions
Understand and redefine the business challenge
Some examples:
A. Dismantle the data
B. Make internal comparisons
C. Make external comparisons
D. Look at changes over time
2
Sift through data and build a knowledge bank
Build answers to the screening questions
One answer per Post-it note
3
Summarize consumer understanding
Combine facts to build nuggets of knowledge
Some examples:
A. Make a logical summary
B. Combine conflicting information
C. Push the boundary
D. Articulate the unsaid

Before applying this to Real Foods, let's consider the three logical steps (see Figure 7.1) that form the backbone of distilling data into useful knowledge.

Ask the Right Screening Questions Based on the Data

This will help you understand and redefine the business challenge. As a starting point, you can:

(A) Dismantle the data
(B) Make internal comparisons
(C) Make external comparisons
(D) Look at changes over time

But these processes are not watertight. If you can think of other logical ways of asking screening questions and compartmentalizing your data, feel free to do that. Remember this is a brainstorming technique; be flexible.

Answer the Screening Questions by Sifting through the Data

Very simply, answer each question on a Post-it note. Once done, write the questions on a flip chart and stick all the Post-it answers to each question below it.

Summarize Consumer Understanding into Nuggets of Knowledge

To do this, move around the Post-it notes to make new clusters that you think make sense. In other words, move the statement from the groups created by the questions into other logical buckets. As you regroup the Post-it notes, feel free to use one statement in more than one group. How? By simply copying that statement on a new Post-it note and sticking it under the new group!

While you're at it, consider grouping Post-it statements by way of:

(A) A logical summary
(B) Combining conflicting information

(C) Pushing the boundary
(D) Articulating the unsaid

Now, let me explain each of these activities using the example of the hypothetical Real Foods.

Figure 7.2 illustrates how best to **ask the right screening questions based on the data,** to address the business challenge of growing the food delivery business.

Figure 7.2 Examples of Screening Questions for Real Foods

Brainstorming Technique	Screening Questions
(A) Dismantle the data	• What are the customer's expectations? • How are these expectations being met today? • What are some of the operational challenges of a delivery service? • What are some of the operating efficiencies?
(B) Internal comparisons	• How is our take-out business doing? Is it growing? • What do consumers say about it? • At what time of the day is the delivery service being used the most? • When is it being used the least?
(C) External comparisons	• Who is doing the best job of delivery in the food business? And what can we learn from them? • Who is doing the best job of delivery outside the restaurant business? And what can we learn from them?
(D) Changes over time	• How has food delivery been growing as an industry? And what's the projected growth for the next five years? • How is delivery outside the food industry growing? And what's the projected growth over the next five years? • What are the consumer trends in the areas of convenience and super-convenience?

★

To illustrate how **to answer the screening questions by sifting through data**, let's look at the first two questions under *(A) Dismantle the data,* and try answering them:

What are the customer's expectations?
The customer is primarily looking for convenience—food that can be ordered easily and delivered within a reasonable amount of time. Food quality is next on the priority list—however, customers understand that food delivered at home won't be as fresh, hot, and tasty as food consumed at a dine-in. So they're willing to pay more specifically for the convenience of food delivery.

How are these expectations being met today?
There are multiple causes for customer dissatisfaction—among them, being told that their residence is 'outside the service area' and cannot be catered to ('Why advertise a delivery service then?' the customer typically asks). In many cases, consumers are unhappy with the delivery time but, if it is going to take an hour, they'd rather be told that upfront. They feel cheated of their money when they're made to wait longer than they bargained for.

Since the aim is to show you how brainstorming works, I don't need to take you through the answers for all the questions for Real Foods. However, you must take the time to respond to *every* question exhaustively when you're considering your own business, with a team of people (in groups of five to eight) working on each step.

★

Next, in the Real Foods example, to **summarize consumer understanding into 'nuggets of knowledge'**, we may come up with a group called 'value for money'. Into this group we may move statements like: 'People are willing to pay more for the convenience of food delivery' and 'They feel cheated of their money when they're made to wait for longer than they've bargained for'—statements listed as answers to two different screening questions. Similarly we may add more statements to this group from the answers to the other screening questions. We might also have other groups like 'convenience' and 'marketing communication', to name just two.

Through divergence we have opened an arena of possibilities. It is now time for convergence. Once we have all the statements clustered in various groups like 'value for money', 'convenience', 'marketing communication', and so on, the task is to use them to develop meaningful statements. To help you with brainstorming at the stage of convergence, consider (a) making logical summaries, (b) combining conflicting information, (c) pushing boundaries, and (d) articulating the unsaid. The resulting nuggets of knowledge are stepping stones to the final insight; in fact, these statements often begin to sound like insights. If you stumble upon a full-fledged insight at this stage, accept it as a happy bonus!

In the Real Foods case study, **a logical summary** may result in this nugget of knowledge: 'People using a delivery service are paying not just for the food but also for the convenience of having it delivered.' This is not yet an insight but it is pointing in the direction of one . . . and in the next step (covered in the next chapter) you'll see how, when we apply the next set of brainstorming techniques to it, we will arrive at insights!

Similarly, **combining conflicting information** may lead to two more nuggets of knowledge: 'People want value for money but are prepared to pay a premium for the convenience of home delivery' and 'People want hot and fresh food but make a conscious compromise when it comes to home delivery (because of the convenience factor).'

When we try **pushing the boundary** we arrive at these two nuggets of knowledge: 'People who avail of delivery services are willing to wait till the promised delivery time (30 minutes, for example) but get annoyed about every additional minute they're made to wait' and 'People place such a premium on time that they hate it when it is wasted.'

And finally, **articulating the unsaid** may lead us to conclude: 'Everything is magnified when you're hungry.' Figure 7.3 offers a summary.

Figure 7.3 Example of Developing Nuggets of Knowledge for Real Foods

Technique	Nuggets of knowledge
Logical summary	1. People using a delivery service are paying not just for the food but also for the convenience of having it delivered.
Combining conflicting information	2. People want value for money but are prepared to pay a premium for the convenience of home delivery. 3. People want hot and fresh food but make a conscious compromise when it comes to home delivery (because of the convenience factor).
Push the boundary	4. People who avail of delivery services are willing to wait till the promised delivery time (30 minutes, for example) but get annoyed about every minute that they're made to wait beyond this. 5. People place such a premium on time that they hate it when it is wasted.
Articulate the unsaid	6. Everything is magnified when you're hungry.

These are examples of six nuggets of knowledge—derived from just a few screening questions—to show you what brainstorming techniques can deliver. In fact, you could argue that the last nugget ('Everything is magnified when you're hungry') is already an insight!

SUMMARY

- Any brand can develop meaningful insights like Dove did by following a simple but rigorous five-step process:
  (1) Articulating the business challenge
  (2) Compiling all the data relevant to this challenge (internal and external)
  (3) Distilling the data into useful knowledge ('nuggets of knowledge')
  (4) Writing insights based on the 'nuggets of knowledge'
  (5) Building full-fledged action plans based on the insights

- It is important to follow time-tested brainstorming techniques and principles while applying this process.
- Brainstorming begins at step 3—distilling data into useful knowledge—where you need to ask the right screening questions; sift through the data to answer the questions and build a knowledge bank; and finally, summarize consumer understanding by writing out the 'nuggets of knowledge'.

Chapter 8
Writing the Insight: Beyond Nuggets of Knowledge

'You can't wait for inspiration. You have to go after it with a club.'
—Jack London

Vicks VapoRub—an ointment that, when applied, offers a warm, soothing sensation and helps ease chest and nose congestion—has always been marketed as effective treatment for a child's cold. That it is mild (compared to harsher rubs and balms in the market) and comes with natural ingredients makes it a safe choice.

P&G acquired Richardson-Vicks in 1985 in a friendly takeover (Groves, 1985), and as a result acquired the flagship VapoRub, among many others brands like Clearasil and Oil of Olay (now Olay).

Over the years, P&G marketers stayed true to VapoRub's advertising heritage—of a concerned mother taking care of her sick child, using the magic ointment, of course. (I can personally confirm that this strategy was consistently deployed based on my many years of managing Vicks in India and the ASEAN region.) For example, a famous VapoRub advertisement that ran for over a decade in India begins with a woman opening her front door during a thunderstorm and finding her young boy outside, drenched. Just then, he sneezes. 'You've got a cold?' she scolds him in Hindi. 'Why did you go out?' The boy hands over a bouquet of flowers he had hidden behind his back and says, 'Happy birthday, Mummy!' She hugs him, her anger forgotten. The ad cuts to her applying VapoRub on the child's chest, back, head, and nose; then it cuts to the next morning when the boy wakes up and takes a deep breath, his cold a distant memory![14]

Other countries employed similar advertising. VapoRub's strategy was consistent and the underlying insight—though not formally articulated in these words in every market—is: 'A mother's love gets heightened when her child is sick.'

Over the years, even while staying true to its strategy and advertising approach, P&G continued to tap into its knowledge about consumers—how they treated coughs and colds at home—and how VapoRub's communication could evolve with this information. Along the way, P&G discovered that there was some medical research suggesting that parents, by touching, comforting, and caring for their ailing children, played an important role in the healing process, augmenting the effectiveness of the actual medicine given.

Based on this knowledge, in the 1990s, P&G Philippines developed an insight for VapoRub: 'A mother's touch helps her sick child recover.' P&G realized it had arrived at a brilliant insight. And when we view it through the three criteria that define an insight, we can easily see why P&G was excited!

1. It is a human revelation—upon reading this statement, mothers, who may have failed to consider their own role in the healing process, will pause and concur.

2. It's definitely relevant to the product category (of medicines for coughs and colds).

3. And finally, the insight is eminently suitable for building the Vicks VapoRub brand. The product *requires* the mother to touch the child. The scientific rationale amplifies the emotional bond between a mother and a sick child, which the brand has always stood for. As a facilitator of the mother-child relationship, the brand becomes something special.

---

14 You can watch the Vicks VapoRub advertisement on Facebook, at <https://www.facebook.com/IndianAdvertisingArchives/videos/10150837977243506/>, accessed on 21 December 2016.

P&G, convinced that it had found the perfect insight, began to leverage it globally.

In the previous chapter, we covered the first three steps of developing insights (shown in Figure 6.1):

1. Articulating the business challenge;
2. Compiling all the data relevant to this challenge (internal and external); and
3. Distilling the data into useful knowledge ('nuggets of knowledge').

In this chapter we will cover step 4, which is nothing but a *systematic way* of doing what the folks in VapoRub did.

Step 4: Writing Insights Based on the 'Nuggets of Knowledge'

The Process

There are three steps to writing insights (see Figure 8.1):

Figure 8.1 The Three Steps to Writing Insights

	The Steps	The Tasks
1	Prioritize nuggets of knowledge from the previous section's output	Simply **rank** all the nuggets of knowledge and decide how many to focus on
2	For each nugget of knowledge, write meaningful consumer statements	Use **curious querying** on each nugget to develop several meaningful consumer statements 1 2 3 4 etc.
3	Write insights based on the consumer statements	Use '**combine, modify, and rewrite**' techniques to develop insights from consumer statements

1. The first step is to select a few nuggets. You could do this by arranging nuggets in descending order of quality—based on your judgement—and choosing how many you would like to work on.
2. Once you have prioritized the nuggets, you take each one and apply the 'curious querying' technique to it. Ask a series of questions and list the answers (each on a separate Post-it note, of course).

Here are the questions. We'll explain each of them later, using Real Foods as a case study.

A) ***Why*** is this (nugget of knowledge) true?

Answer this with a statement. Then ask the same question to the statement: why is *this* true? Keep doing this until you feel you've reached a dead end. Now, note down the statements that sound meaningful and can be built into insights. Sometimes, you may end with an insight that needs little rewriting.

B) ***What else*** is like this?

As humans, we love analogies and metaphors. Rick Wormeli calls them 'power tools' for teaching any subject (Wormeli, 2009). The 'what else is like this' question helps create analogies that can lead to surprisingly strong insights. Since this is a brainstorming technique designed to open your mind, let the creative juices flow and, depending on the nugget of knowledge you're working on, think of more than one analogy if you can.

C) ***How*** does this affect what people think, say, and do?

Articulate each of these three separately.

D) ***What if*** things were different?

Plot out different what-if situations and go whichever way your creativity takes you. As an example, if you were managing a dairy brand and were working on this nugget of knowledge—'Children find milk boring'—you might ask: 'What if milk came in different colours instead of white?' And the answers might reveal some interesting insights, but I'm not going there now!

3. When you have the answers to these probing questions, you are ready to write insights. Some of the statements you have at the end of this questioning exercise may already be insights, requiring little or no rewriting. For the others, take logical leaps to deduce insights, making creative inferences from the statements. This could mean combining, modifying or rewriting them if necessary.

While building knowledge, asking screening questions opens our minds (divergence), and summarizing consumer understanding helps hone in on a few statements (convergence). While writing insights, curious querying opens our minds to different ideas (divergence), and taking logical leaps—by combining, modifying, and rewriting statements—helps us arrive at the best insights (convergence).

Real Foods

In the last chapter, we arrived at six nuggets of knowledge for the hypothetical Real Foods to enter the food delivery market (refer to Figure 7.3). To illustrate how the process of curious querying works, I'm going to select just one nugget: 'People want value for money but are prepared to pay a premium for the convenience of home delivery.'

A. ***Why*** is this (nugget of knowledge) true? In other words:

—***Why*** are people prepared to pay a premium for the convenience of home delivery?

Answer: Because they have no time to cook food or go somewhere to buy it.

—***Why*** don't they have time to cook food or go somewhere to buy it?

Answer: Because the pace of their lives is much faster.

—***Why*** is the pace of their lives much faster?
Answer: Because they demand more from themselves today, and so does society.

I would stop here because that last answer is an insight! Here is how I would articulate it: 'Today, people demand more from themselves and from each other than they ever did.' This sentence captures the pressures we face nowadays—in our jobs; in domestic spaces; and while trying to keep up-to-date with the world and our friends and acquaintances, who (thanks to the power of digital engagement) are numerous. In such a scenario, time management and convenience become vital—and are exactly what food delivery offers. Therefore the insight that people demand more from themselves and from each other can be leveraged by Real Foods.

Remember, we're not judging whether this insight is the best or even great. That will come later. At this stage we're generating insights—as many as we can.

A word of caution: just because I asked you to stop probing on approaching a potential insight doesn't mean you should, especially if you're brainstorming within a group. Continue asking 'why'—for instance, *why* do people expect more from themselves and each other? You might answer this by saying: 'Because technology has made it easy, necessary even, for us to multitask.' This might lead you to an insight in the area of 'multitasking'. And therein lies the power of this process!

★

B. ***What else*** is like this? In other words:
—***What else*** are people willing to pay a little extra for, for added convenience?
Answer: A booking fee for buying movie tickets online, or a booking fee for calling a taxi to the doorstep and not searching for it. (I could go on but two are enough to make the point.)

Here, I will take the *logical leap* of saying that today, hectic schedules have made saving time especially critical for people. I express this through the insight: 'Time is the most valuable currency for today's NOW generation.'

—***What else,*** besides conveniences, are people willing to pay a little extra for?

Answer: A premium on an economy class flight ticket for extra leg-room, or a foot massage after a hard day.

The *logical leap* here leads to an insight: 'If I'm saving money to enjoy things, why not enjoy them now?'

The first insight offers a penetrating revelation about today's ESCAPE-ing consumer who is starved for time. It can also be leveraged by the category of food service, especially delivery—in this instance, by Real Foods.

The second insight also offers a human revelation, especially pertinent to the millennials—about the need to live life now. However, it seems to have little connection with our category of food service and delivery. Most likely, it will not make it to the shortlist of insights we choose for Real Foods, but we'll come to that later.

For now let's earmark these as two more potential insights for Real Foods from the same nugget of knowledge.

★

C. ***How*** does this affect what people ***think, say,*** and ***do***? In other words:

—***How does*** the demand for saving time affect what people ***think***?

Answer: People think they've been cheated if they book a table at a restaurant and it's not ready when they enter. (This is obviously not the only answer possible, let alone the best one! But it's up to you to answer the question the way you like.)

—***How*** does the demand for saving time affect what ***people say***?
Answer: People say, 'I feel frustrated if I have to spend even a minute doing nothing.'

—***How*** does the demand for saving time affect what ***people do***?
Answer: People consult an app that informs them about the arrival time of their bus at their bus stop before stepping out of their homes (so that they don't have to wait more than a minute at the bus stop).

Based on these answers, I would make *logical leaps* to write the following insights:

— 'If they're not doing anything, people panic because they think they're wasting their lives.'
— 'The irritation caused by a five-minute delay today is comparable to the irritation caused by a two-hour delay 15 years ago.'

You can pause to examine how these two statements express your sentiments or those of someone you know. You will agree that they're both applicable to a situation of someone waiting for food to be delivered. Let's add them to our shortlist of potential insights.

★

D. ***What if*** things were different? In other words:
—***What if*** there were no delivery services at all for anything?
Answer: People would think they were back in the Jurassic era.

—***What if*** food could be delivered in five minutes instead of 30?
Answer: —People would be ecstatic;
—People would be willing to pay double.

I then make a *logical leap* to write this insight: 'Saving a few minutes today is more important than saving a few dollars.'

That's another revelation with respect to today's time-starved consumer that is certainly applicable to food delivery and could therefore potentially be used by Real Foods. Now you may think that this is similar to an insight uncovered earlier, namely: 'Time is the most valuable currency for today's NOW generation', and you would be right. But I will deal with this at the step of collating and evaluating insights.

The curious querying exercise we just did for Real Foods is summarized in Figure 8.2.

While studying the insights in the last column—impressively, half a dozen of them—we should remind ourselves that they're drawn from just one nugget of knowledge!

Now, all these insights are not equally powerful and they may not all be relevant to the business challenge. Your task is to select the very best that will address your business challenge, and you'll see how to do this in the next chapter.

Figure 8.2 Example of Developing Nuggets of Knowledge for Real Foods

Question		**Answer**	**Insight**
A.	**Why is this true?**		
	Why are people prepared to pay a premium for the convenience of home delivery?	Because they have no time to cook food or go somewhere to buy it.	**1. 'Today, people demand more from themselves and from each other than they ever did.'**
	Why don't they have time to cook food or go somewhere to buy it?	Because the pace of their lives is much faster.	
	Why is the pace of their lives much faster?	Because they demand more from themselves today, and so does society.	
B.	**What else is like this?**		
	What else are people willing to pay a little extra for, for added convenience?	A booking fee for buying movie tickets online, or a booking fee for calling a taxi to the doorstep and not searching for it.	**2. 'Time is the most valuable currency for today's NOW generation.'**

	What else, besides conveniences, are people willing to pay a little extra for?	A premium on an economy class flight ticket for extra leg-room, or a foot massage after a hard day.	**3. 'If I'm saving money to enjoy things, why not enjoy them now?'**
C.	**How does this affect what people think, say, and do?**		
	How does the demand for saving time affect what people think?	People think they've been cheated if they book a table at a restaurant and it's not ready when they enter.	**4. 'If they're not doing anything, people panic because they think they're wasting their lives.'**
	How does the demand for saving time affect what people say?	People say, 'I feel frustrated if I have to spend even a minute doing nothing.'	
	How does this demand for saving time affect what people do?	People consult an app that informs them about the arrival time of their bus at their bus stop before stepping out of their homes (so that they don't have to wait more than a minute at the bus stop).	**5. 'The irritation caused by a five-minute delay today is like that caused by a two-hour delay 15 years ago.'**
D.	**What if things were different?**		
	What if there were no delivery services at all for anything?	People would think they are back in the Jurassic era.	**6. 'Saving a few minutes today is more important than saving a few dollars.'**
	What if food could be delivered in five minutes instead of 30?	—People would be ecstatic; —People would be willing to pay double.	

SUMMARY

- Writing insights based on the 'nuggets of knowledge' (step 4 in the process) relies on divergence and convergence.
- Take one nugget at a time and use the brainstorming technique of asking four questions (the 'curious querying' technique) and answering them with creative abandon (divergence):
  - Why is this true?
  - What else is like this?
  - How does this affect what people think, say, and do?
  - What if things could be different?
- Take logical leaps (combining, modifying, and rewriting the statements, as required) to arrive at insights (convergence).

Chapter 9
Selecting the Best Insights: Evaluations

'I must have a prodigious quantity of mind; it takes me as much as a week sometimes to make it up.'
—Mark Twain

We've now gone through the first four steps in the process of developing insights—ending with how to write insights from nuggets of knowledge. Before getting to step 5—building full-fledged action plans based on insights—I'd like to cover how to select the best insights from the ones you've written. Our objective is to identify those insights that are *best* suited to our brand and the business challenge it faces, the ones that will increase its mental availability and therefore deliver long-term growth.

How to Evaluate Insights

There are three ways to assess insights.

Identification

Identification tests how well an insight fits within the first part of my definition of the word: 'an emotional *human revelation* relevant to the category that is leveraged to build a brand'. In other words, how strong is the human revelation? Does it create empathy with target consumers? How likely are they to react to it saying, 'Yes, exactly!', 'I so get it!' or 'This could be me!'?

Many of the insights we discussed—for instance, 'In times of stress people seek comfort in the familiar' (McDonald's) and 'Dirt is good for kids to develop' (Omo)—have strong identification. When you stumble upon an insight of this kind, you're on to a good thing, and should move on to the next criterion.

Relevance

Now, ask how relevant an insight (with strong identification) is to the category. If it is irrelevant, you need to abandon it, albeit reluctantly! For example, while working on the branding of a fruit-filled cereal targeting the parents of little children, you may generate the insight: 'For many people a dog is more a child than a pet.' It's a great revelation, with strong 'identification', but you need to let it go because it's not germane to the category.

Inspiration

Finally, ask: does the insight have creative potential? Will it lend itself well not just to ad campaigns but also to ideas related to product, promotions, activation, and so on? Can it be leveraged for a long time?

A word of caution: while you examine an insight for 'inspiration', refrain from rejecting it outright if it fails to inspire multiple ideas across different touchpoints or if it cannot be used for a long time. It's fine to go with an insight that can only be used via one medium (say television) or can be leveraged merely for a short period of time, if you believe it makes a strong emotional connection that's relevant to the category (that is, if it scores brilliantly against the first two criteria).

A good example is an endearing McDonald's television ad about a man driving around a drive-through lane late at night without stopping at the takeaway window; rather, he hurriedly shouts out his order every time he passes it. The attendant is puzzled at first, then notices a baby sleeping in the back seat. Immediately, the restaurant team rallies around to meet the father's order—using a note on the window to tell him how much to pay, handing him the food, and collecting his money while he is on the move.[15]

The insight—'Parents will go to ridiculous lengths to keep their sleeping baby asleep, including not stopping their moving car'—is a simple observation about human behaviour, but one that comes with strong identification. And nothing is more relevant to a drive-through service than a moving car! In other words, this insight does very well against the first two criteria. But it cannot be used for very long.[16] Besides, it probably will act as a very weak advertisement in print or in any medium besides television. In other words, the insight falls short on 'inspiration'. But it's still a great one-off television campaign opportunity, and for this reason, McDonald's went ahead and used the insight!

An afterthought regarding the way the insight has been phrased. I could have stopped at: 'Parents will go to ridiculous lengths to keep their sleeping baby asleep.' But how is this relevant to a drive-through restaurant? It's only when we add the words, '. . . including not stopping their moving car', that we establish a firm connection between the insight and the category. (To refresh your memory, this also explains the choice of words for the insight guiding Omo—'Getting dirty is good for children to develop.' Instead of suggesting, 'Being spontaneous, playing, exploring the world, having fun, and just being kids help children grow into happy, whole adults', Omo chose to define its insight narrowly because 'getting dirty' is relevant to the detergent category.)

---

15 You can watch the McDonald's ad on YouTube, at <https://www.youtube.com/watch?v=3LJvV4dHtHA>, accessed on 16 December 2016.

16 This insight is a great way to showcase the delightful experience the McDonald's crew offers—in this case by enthusiastically accommodating the father's strange behaviour (and thus highlighting the convenience of its drive-through service). But McDonald's needs to show other situations (in the drive-through service and in the restaurant) where the crew go the extra mile; it cannot rely only on one episode of them meeting the needs of a parent disinclined to stop a car and wake a child!

Evaluating the Real Foods Insights

Let's apply these three criteria to evaluate the six insights in the Real Foods example.

1. 'Today, people demand more from themselves and from each other than they ever did.'

Instead of focusing on the functional aspects of delivery (speed and ease of use), this insight will allow Real Foods to show that it understands why time management is important for consumers. It opens a rich territory—the brand gets to make an emotional connection! It ticks all the three boxes of identification, relevance, and inspiration.

Now let's list three of the remaining five insights (this is not the original order).

2. 'Time is the most valuable currency for today's NOW generation.'

3. 'Saving a few minutes today is more important than saving a few dollars.'

4. 'The irritation caused by a five-minute delay today is like that caused by a two-hour delay 15 years ago.'

I grouped these insights together because they're related. All come with strong identification—people value time and are not happy wasting it—and are relevant—a food delivery category is all about saving time.

Insight 2—'Time is the most valuable currency for today's NOW generation'—is a broad one and I would therefore shortlist that as the key insight. But the other two statements (3 and 4) add texture to it. So what do I do? Simple—I use them all!

Here's how I will write the insight in its full verbose glory: 'Time is the most valuable currency for today's NOW generation.

For example, people value saving a few minutes more than saving a few dollars. And they get more irritated with a five-minute delay than their parents did with a two-hour delay 15 years ago.' It's prolix, but since the consumer won't see the full statement, we don't have to worry about it.

Now, let's consider the two insights that remain:

5. 'If they're not doing anything, people panic because they think they're wasting their lives.'

Most would agree with this ('identification') and it can spark creative ideas ('inspiration'). But is it truly germane to the delivery business ('relevance')? I don't think so. Real Foods may not be able to leverage it in a powerful way. Therefore I'm dropping it.

6. 'If I'm saving money to enjoy things, why not do it now?'

Even more than the previous example, this insight—while being a human revelation and having creative potential—does not hold much relevance. I would not pursue it for a delivery brand like Real Foods.

I should add a caveat: if Real Foods were a real company and the team working on developing insights felt differently about statements 5 and 6, I would urge them to rely on their judgement!

Finally, to round off the chapter, a point of observation. In my experience, people fall into three categories with respect to their attitude to insights:

—Insight-ignorers don't look for an insight at all.

—Insight-recognizers don't actively seek out an insight but are happy to use it if it comes along as part of the creative process (in other words, they leave it to chance).

—Insight-seekers work hard to get an insight as part of the brand development and creative processes.

Become an insight-seeker!

SUMMARY

- The three criteria to evaluate an insight are:
  (1) Identification: the strength of its human revelation.
  (2) Relevance: its link to the category.
  (3) Inspiration: its power to spawn ideas across media and over time.
- While every insight should have strong 'identification' and 'relevance', we may sometimes choose insights that are necessarily short-lived or cannot come to life across multiple media (that is, those weak on 'inspiration').
- Don't be an insight-ignorer or -recognizer. Grow into an insight-seeker.

Chapter 10
The Insight Action Plan: Ideas and Tactics

'The value of an idea lies in the using of it.'
—Thomas Edison

At the end of step 4 (writing insights based on the 'nuggets of knowledge') you should have one or two powerful insights that you and your team are excited about. But insights themselves are of little value unless you bring them to life. Thus, the fifth and last step in our process—building full-fledged action plans based on the insights—will be the focus of this chapter.

I recommend a simple framework (Figure 10.1) and that you transfer the work you've done so far (in steps 1 to 4) into it.

Is it the *only* framework that you might use? Good lord, no! There are probably as many frameworks in existence as there are consulting firms and advertising agencies! Figure 10.1 highlights only one of the many you could exploit.

If you analyze Figure 10.1, you'll see that the **challenge** is followed by the **context**—which is a brief description of the competitive landscape your brand must navigate to address the challenge or the opportunity, and grow. Then comes the **insight**—the central component of the insight action plan, the part that will make it come to life—which, I sincerely hope, you are now familiar with. This is followed by the **brand benefit**—the long-term positioning of the brand—and the **big idea**—how the benefit will be brought to life against the insight in this campaign. Finally come **tactics**—you could also call this the marketing plan or the 4P (product, price, place, and promotion) plan—which help activate the big idea. Advertising can be an important part of tactics, but it need not be the only thing. A good insight can steer more than the brand's communication—it can inspire product, promotion, activation, endorsement, and other ideas.

Figure 10.1 A Framework for Developing the Insight Action Plan

Challenge
The business opportunity defined succinctly
Context
Challenges faced in the category, including competition
Insight
An emotional human revelation relevant to the category leveraged to build the brand
Brand Benefit
The functional and emotional benefit of the brand
Big Idea
A powerful idea based on the insight, within the category context, leveraging brand benefit and addressing the business challenge
Tactics
A range of programmes and tactics to bring the big idea to life

Case Studies

I'm now going to show you how the framework we've discussed operates through two examples—Dove and Snickers. A word of caution: these are my deductions about the two brands and they have been arranged into my framework. The brands themselves have not used this framework to describe their strategy.

Dove

Let's start with Dove. In response to its business challenge of transforming itself from a gentle soap into a beauty masterbrand, Dove came up with a number of tactics:

1. It created a 'Self-esteem Fund' designed to make young girls—the most vulnerable victims of the false notions of beauty being perpetrated by other beauty brands—feel better about themselves. The fund was 'committed to reaching five million young women by the end of 2010' and financing 'selected projects and organisations in a large number of countries around the world'[17] (Herrera, 2012).

2. To launch the fund, Dove created a memorable television campaign called 'True Colors', which shows young girls, with snippets of their insecurities appearing as text below them ('hates her freckles', 'thinks she's ugly', 'wishes she were blonde', and so on). The ad ends with a call to stop this form of persecution and help girls feel good about themselves.[18]

3. Dove followed this up with a 'Campaign for Real Beauty' across multiple media—television, outdoor, internet, and print.

4. Not only were other brands showcasing models as symbols of perfect beauty, but they were also using makeup and computer touch-up effects to significantly enhance the models' looks. Dove exposed this practice through a short film referred to as 'Evolution'—where a model's face dramatically transforms under the expert care of makeup artists and touch-up experts, and is only then advertised. The campaign was posted on YouTube with the hope that it would go viral. And it did, receiving over 18 million views![19]

5. A few years later, Dove followed this up with another viral campaign called 'Sketches'[20] that was even more popular

---

17 More here: 'Dove: The Campaign for Real Beauty and Dove Self-Esteem Fund', at <http://sofii.org/case-study/dove-campaign-for-real-beauty-and-dove-self-esteem-fund>, accessed on 15 December 2016.

18 You can watch Dove's 'True Colors' campaign on YouTube, at <https://www.youtube.com/watch?v=tUA8PvLsZgU>, accessed on 16 December 2016.

19 You can watch Dove's 'Evolution' on YouTube, at <https://www.youtube.com/watch?v=iYhCn0jf46U>, accessed on 16 December 2016.

20 You can watch Dove's 'Sketches' on YouTube, at <https://www.youtube.com/watch?v=XpaOjMXyJGk>, accessed on 19 December 2016.

(over 66 million views). It movingly demonstrates the average woman's poor perception of her own beauty compared to how others view her. A forensic artist sketches a woman based on her description of herself and then repeats the exercise based on a relative stranger's description. The result is dramatic—each woman in the experiment looks far more beautiful in the picture drawn according to the stranger's description than her own. The ad ends with the words, 'You are more beautiful than you think', bringing Dove's big idea to life in a memorable way.

6. Recently, Dove launched an 'Ad Makeover' on Facebook, where Dove outbid brands targeting vulnerable women who 'need' beauty aids (women who think they're overweight, dark, not beautiful, and so on) with positive messages that enhanced each woman's perception of beauty.[21]

Dove is a great example of a brand that has shaped its entire strategy around a very powerful insight. Figure 10.2 summarizes Dove's approach within my insight action plan framework.

Figure 10.2 Dove's Insight Action Plan

Challenge	**Relaunch Dove as a 'beauty brand' as against pitching it as a 'white soap'.**
Context	**Dove is seen as a soap associated with simplicity and gentleness. The beauty category is highly competitive, with many new products being launched every year.**
Insight	**Women don't consider themselves beautiful because beauty brands have assailed them with false definitions of beauty: size zero, blonde, flawless, toned, young, etc.**
Brand Benefit = Big Idea	**Dove champions real beauty which goes beyond 'model' looks.**
Tactics	**• 'Self-esteem Fund' for girls to feel betteer about themselves • 'True Colors' campaign to launch the Self-esteem Fund • 'Campaign for Real Beauty' across TV, print, internet, outdoors, etc • 'Evolution' viral campaign on 'how a model is manufactured' • 'Sketches' campaign to highlight women's poor perception of their beauty • Facebook 'Ad Makeover' campaign (supplanting ads targeting women's insecurity with Dove's positive messages)**

21 You can watch the Dove 'Ad Makeover' on YouTube, at <https://www.youtube.com/watch?v=818if1bkCdo>, accessed on 19 December 2016.

Dove believed in its insight enough to build a long-term brand strategy around it. I've articulated this by using the same statement for Dove's big idea and benefit ('Dove champions real beauty which goes beyond "model" looks'). If your brand is similarly committed to an insight, by all means combine the benefit and big idea. As you can see from Figure 10.2, the template can flexibly accommodate this.

Snickers

In other cases, the big idea may be how the brand addresses an insight *now*, within its long-term brand benefit. At some other time, it may focus on *another* insight, leading to one more big idea, both still in sync with the long-term brand benefit. Snickers could fit into the second category. Let me try to deduce the insight action plan based on Snickers' campaign.

Snickers, a ready-to-eat packaged chocolate bar, faced the **business challenge** of re-establishing its brand as a hunger satisfaction solution. It had to do so in a highly competitive market, fighting not just other packaged snacks, but also fast-food restaurants, vending machines, street vendors, beverages, desserts, and so on—that's the **context**. To achieve this end, the **insight** that Snickers decided to focus on for its campaign was: 'When very hungry, genuinely nice people can become disagreeable.'

Admittedly, this is a great insight. After all, who hasn't displayed uncharacteristic irritation when famished? The emotion is relevant to the category. In fact, the word 'hungry' is at the heart of the revelation! So, it can definitely be leveraged by Snickers.

And Snickers did this with flair by advertising its **brand benefit**—that it is a 'tasty, handheld snack that gives quick energy on-the-go'. A group is shown travelling in a car; the woman in the back seat gets cranky and starts complaining about things. The young man next to her gives her Snickers, saying, 'Every time you're hungry, you become a diva. Just eat this so we can all coexist.' The woman takes a bite, and transforms into a young, cheerful man. One then realizes that hunger had transformed him into a disagreeable prima donna.[22] Clearly, the **big idea** is: 'Snickers transforms you back to your real you!'

However, the power of this insight and big idea can go beyond advertising. So, under **tactics,** I've listed a few creative ideas on my own:

1. In addition to television advertising, Snickers could also tap into the 'targeting' offered by the digital medium. It could remind presumably hungry internet surfers about its insight. For example, a Snickers ad band could appear alongside food reviews, recipes, and so on.

2. Snickers' bite-sized packages could be exploited to make its benefit and big idea—'Tasty energy on-the-go that transforms you back to your real you'—come alive easily, quickly, and anywhere.

3. Snickers could introduce vending machines at all transit hubs like bus stops and railway stations, so people can get themselves the fuel needed to 'stay true to themselves' over the long journey and ensure that hunger doesn't transform them into unlikeable souls.

4. Snickers could partner with Snapchat and create a branded filter that transforms people into disagreeable caricatures when they're hungry. Consumers could either post it as a Snickers story on what hunger can do, or share it with their friends!

5. Snickers could sponsor a spoof programme on 'hunger-anger management'.

While, in real life, Snickers does have vending machines, is available in bite-size packaging, and showcases multiple ads based on its insight, I don't believe I've seen the other ideas executed—and maybe they should be! Snickers' hypothetical insight action plan is shown in Figure 10.3.

---

22 You can watch the Snickers campaign on YouTube, at <https://www.youtube.com/watch?v=vW6ZXHWvaGc>, accessed on 19 December 2016.

Figure 10.3 Snickers' Insight Action Plan

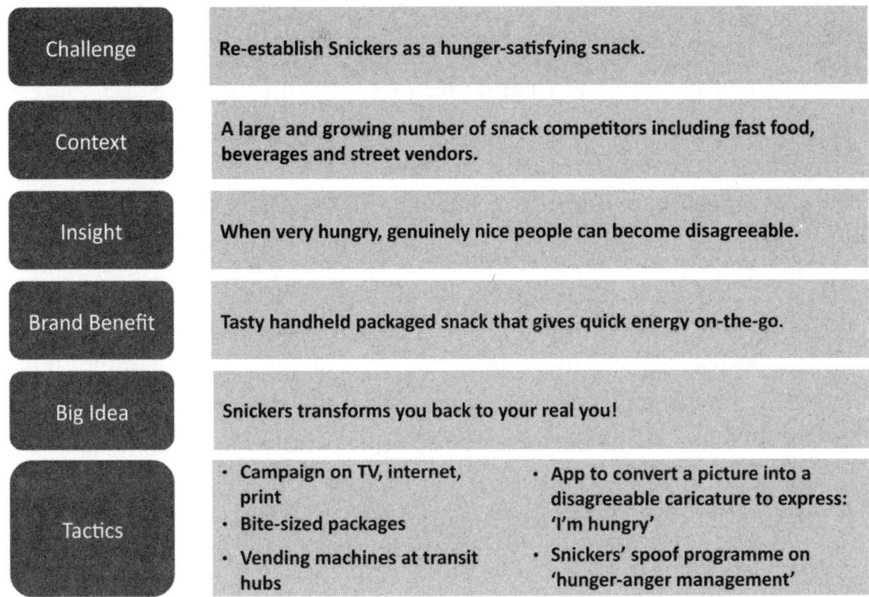

Challenge
Re-establish Snickers as a hunger-satisfying snack.
Context
A large and growing number of snack competitors including fast food, beverages and street vendors.
Insight
When very hungry, genuinely nice people can become disagreeable.
Brand Benefit
Tasty handheld packaged snack that gives quick energy on-the-go.
Big Idea
Snickers transforms you back to your real you!
Tactics
• Campaign on TV, internet, print
• Bite-sized packages
• Vending machines at transit hubs
• App to convert a picture into a disagreeable caricature to express: 'I'm hungry'
• Snickers' spoof programme on 'hunger-anger management'

Now, Snickers could well stick to its insight and big idea for the long run. However, it *could* also move to a different insight and big idea to convey the same brand benefit. As a hypothetical example, to illustrate the point, being a 'tasty snack that gives energy on-the-go' (brand benefit), Snickers could develop the insight—'Snacking gives people some respite during a lousy day'—and get behind the big idea—'Snickers puts a smile into hunger.'

Real Foods

Let me go back to the example of the Real Foods delivery case study—for which the **challenge, context,** and **insights** have already been listed in preceding chapters—and try to develop an insight action plan for it.

You will recall that we had six insights to choose from (refer to Figure 8.2). Let us assume that we choose the second insight about the value of time in people's lives today. Expressed in its full, wordy version, this insight, you will recall, is: 'Time is the most valuable currency for today's NOW generation.' For example, people value saving a few minutes more than saving a few dollars. And they get more irritated with a five-minute delay today than their parents did with a two-hour delay 15 years ago.'

Marry this with the **brand benefit**—Real Foods ensures that good meals get delivered at the doorstep—and you arrive at the **big idea:** 'Our food . . . at your time.'

I've listed three **tactics** to leverage this big idea.

1. Real Foods could promise to deliver within a specific time frame (say, 45 minutes) and reduce the customer's bill by one dollar for every minute of delay beyond this. (For example, if delivery takes place in one hour, $15 will be deducted from the bill.) This could become the central promise of Real Foods' delivery service in print advertising, on its website, in out-of-home (OOH) locations, on the radio, and so on. By paying people for the time wasted—in other words, by recognizing the dollar value of a consumer's time—Real Foods directly addresses this part of the insight: 'People value saving a few minutes more than saving a few dollars.'

2. Real Foods could also offer delivery at the exact time that the customer desires—not a minute before or after. And it could specify this through an easy ordering system on an app. If it has the courage to go all the way, it could promise 'free delivery if we're more than five minutes off the mark'. This strategy addresses another part of the insight statement—'People get more irritated with a five-minute delay today than their parents did with a two-hour delay 15 years ago.'

3. Real Foods could develop a creative campaign around the big idea—'Our food . . . at your time'—leveraging the main insight: 'Time is the most valuable currency for today's NOW generation.'

What would the advertising look like for Real Foods if we were to leverage the third tactic?

Well, let's not get ahead of ourselves. I'll cover how this idea can be translated into advertising (via a creative brief) in Part 3 of the book!

Figure 10.4 has a snapshot of the hypothetical insight action plan for the hypothetical Real Foods brand.

Figure 10.4 Real Foods' Insight Action Plan

Challenge	**Develop and grow the delivery business of the restaurant.**
Context	**Propelled by the consumers' need for convenience, the delivery market—for food and other items—is growing. Real Foods has a real opportunity to become a significant player here.**
Insight	**Time is the most valuable currency for today's NOW generation.**
Brand Benefit	**Delicious meals delivered at your doorstep.**
Big Idea	**Our food . . . at your time.**
Tactics (a few examples)	• **45-minute delivery guarantee—'We promise to pay $1 for every minute of delay'—highlighted in websites, print, OOH, etc.** • **An app to pre-order meals to be delivered at the exact time you desire (or get your money back).** • **An advertising campaign based on the big idea: 'Our . . . at your time.'**

SUMMARY

- An insight action plan is a simple template outlining the business challenge, context, insight, brand benefit, big idea, and tactics.
- The team as a whole should develop the big idea and the tactics that can be used—with Dove, Snickers, and (the hypothetical) Real Foods acting as relevant case studies.

PART THREE

Creativity That Drives Brand Growth

Chapter 11
Insight-driven Advertising and Brand Building: The Growth Guarantor

'Creativity has the power to transform human behaviour.'
—Leo Burnett

'Creativity is a luxury!' said Christopher Armitage, thumping the table for emphasis. 'What I need are campaigns that bring consumers into our restaurant to buy our food!'

I introduced Real Foods, a fictitious fast food restaurant chain, in Part 2 of the book to illustrate concepts. Well, in Part 3, I'd like to introduce Christopher Armitage, the fictitious managing director of Real Foods in a country in Asia. Since I've had versions of this conversation with several business leaders over the years, please read this as a true account, only with identities camouflaged.

Armitage was a tall, bulky fast-food veteran, having spent the last 19 years in this industry, mostly in restaurant operations. Before being promoted to managing director, he had been the operations director in another Real Foods market. The fact that he had no background or experience in marketing did not dampen his confidence while discussing the subject with me.

Armitage was reacting to what I had just shown him—examples of brilliant creative campaigns that had (positively) changed the course of brands. We were discussing Real Foods' dismal business performance—the brand had seen brief spikes intermittently in response to specific promotions, but these had done nothing to arrest its overall negative trend.

'And to ensure we get such campaigns and turn around the business,' Armitage continued, 'I've become personally involved in marketing. I've signed off every campaign for the past several months!'

No wonder they're terrible, I thought. Many business leaders like Armitage understand marketing *strategy* but have no expertise in *creative development*. However, they don't realize this shortcoming; worse, they don't believe that creative development requires any expertise! In their view, this is 'fun activity' that the marketing team dabbles in and that their role is to inject 'practical business sense' into it.

'We chose to focus on Jumbo Rock this quarter,' said Armitage. Jumbo Rock was Real Foods' signature burger. 'Our analysis shows that only a small percentage of our target consumers are aware of Jumbo Rock and even fewer have ever tried it. But those who have tasted it love the burger, rating it highly on all parameters and commenting on its unique taste.'

I nodded. I liked the logic of focusing on the Jumbo Rock.

'My marketing director wanted to push for brand advertising celebrating its iconic taste,' said Armitage.

I nodded some more. This was beginning to sound like a good marketing story.

'She told me the insight for the advertising was: "People will sometimes go through a lot of trouble to enjoy their favourite food."'

It looked like I wouldn't have to stop nodding.

'I told her, "Let me give you an insight: Your job is to *sell* Jumbo Rocks, and *that* advertising is not going to do it. We need a call-to-action campaign with a commercial message."'

I stopped nodding.

'What was the commercial message?' I asked.

'Buy-one-get-one-free (BOGOF) offer on Jumbo Rocks for one month. Customers responded very positively.'

Of course they did! They would have responded even better to buy-one-get-*two*-free Jumbo Rocks.

'How were sales the following month?' I asked.

'Not so good.'

Now, I'd like to take you back to Chapter 2, where we looked at the role of temporary price discounts in the space of packaged goods. Through empirical evidence, we learnt that that the bulk of promotion-buyers are current users and that there is, therefore, no long-term impact with short-term price discounts—in other words, no new users are recruited.

Coming back to Armitage, he was reflecting the built-in bias in the retail industry towards promotions because of short-term sales pressure. A temporary sales spike can come at a huge cost when the promotion is BOGOF or another form of steep price discount. But this cost is often ignored because of accounting practices. Let me explain with—I issue a fair warning—a bit of mathematics.

Say, Real Foods has 200 restaurants in Armitage's country, each of which generates 1,000 transactions a day on average. That's around 6 million transactions a month across the country. Let's assume Armitage's target gross profit (which is the selling price minus the direct cost) is minimum 65 per cent of sales, ideally above 67 per cent.

Jumbo Rock accounts for 5 per cent of all transactions, bringing its transactions to 300,000 per month. Each Jumbo Rock burger is priced at $4. Therefore, in a month, Jumbo Rock's sales is $1.2 million. Assuming the direct cost (food and packaging mainly) is $1.20, each Jumbo Rock then delivers $2.80 in gross profit, which is 70 per cent of sales, comfortably higher than the 65 per cent minimum set by Armitage.

For simplicity, let's assume that the average transaction generates $4 (the same as the sale of one Jumbo Rock burger). So, total sales in a month without a promotion is $24 million and, to keep it simple, the gross profit in such a 'clean, promotion-free' month is 70 per cent, i.e., $16.8 million.

Now, let us say the BOGOF promotion on Jumbo Rock causes its transactions to triple—from 300,000 to 900,000. To continue in that vein of generosity, let's assume that none of this is at the expense of other sales, and that there is no increase in other direct costs during this promotion (costs related to labour, utilities, rent, and so on). Effectively then, during the BOGOF promotion, Jumbo Rock's selling price drops by two dollars (from $4 to $2) and so does the gross profit, bringing it from $2.80 to $0.80 (from 70 per cent to 40 per cent).

Figure 11.1 captures the impact of such a promotion.

Figure 11.1 Sales and Profit Impact of a BOGOF Promotion on Jumbo Rock

Base Data			
A	No. of restaurants		200
B	Average transactions per restaurant per day without promotions		1,000
C	Total monthly transactions (all restaurants, no promotion)	*C = A x B x 30*	6,000,000
D	Total monthly sales (all restaurants, no promotion)	*D = C x $4*	$24,000,000

Promotion Analysis						
			Normal Month	**BOGOF Month**	**Difference $**	**Difference %**
E	Monthly transactions	*E = G + L*	6,000,000	6,600,000	$600,000	10%
F	Sales per month (average transaction at $4)	*F = J + M*	$24,000,000	$24,600,000	$600,000	3%
G	Jumbo Rock transactions (5% total in typical month; 3x during BOGOF)		300,000	900,000	$600,000	200%
H	Jumbo Rock transactions % (to total)	*H = G ÷ E*	5%	14%		
I	Jumbo Rock price per unit		$4.00	$2.00	($2)	-50%
J	Jumbo Rock sales per month	*J = I x G*	$1,200,000	$1,800,000	$600,000	50%

K	Jumbo Rock sales % (to total)	$K = J \div F$	5.0%	7.3%		
L	Transactions without Jumbo Rock (95% of non-promo month transactions)	$L = C \times 95\%$	5,700,000	5,700,000		
M	Sales without Jumbo Rock (average transaction at $4)	$M = L \times \$4$	22,800,000	22,800,000		
N	Gross profit without Jumbo Rock (assumed 70% of sales)	$N = M \times 70\%$	15,960,000	15,960,000		
O	Jumbo Rock gross profit (assuming unit cost of $1.20)	$O = I - \$1.20$	$2.80	$0.80	($2)	-71%
P	Jumbo Rock gross margin (% of sales)	$P = O \div I$	70%	40%		
Q	Jumbo Rock monthly profit	$Q = O \times G$	840,000	720,000	($120,000)	-14%
R	Total gross profit ($)	$R = N + Q$	16,800,000	16,680,000	($120,000)	-1%
S	Overall gross margin (% of sales)	$Q = R \div F$	70%	68%	($0)	-3%

While Jumbo Rock's transactions have tripled and this has increased overall transactions (because of our generous assumption of no cannibalization), the overall sales have only risen by 3 per cent (because of the half price). But more disturbing, the total profit and the gross profit percentage have both dropped.

Now, I've been liberal with my assumptions. If, in actual fact, the gross margin of Jumbo Rock were lower than 70 per cent; if we did not grow transactions by a factor of three (from 300,000 to 900,000); and if some of that growth came at the expense of existing sales, the profit impact would only be worse, ending with an overall gross profit lower than 68 per cent.

So why does Armitage still run this promotion? Well, I believe it's because, despite the discount, the overall gross profit is well above his minimum target and even higher than his ideal. But in a 'promotion-free month' the profit would be 70 per cent, you say? Yes, but such a month may not actually exist! There may always be some activity—discounts, special meal deals, coupons for redemption, new products launched (at a lower gross profit), and so on.

By 'managing' the business to a gross profit target, I believe many retailers get away with doing frequent promotions. Such promotions may erode profitability and they may be effectively paying for incremental sales with lost profit—but as long as the overall profit is within target, no explanation is required. In other words, although the role of price-discount promotions is dubious, accounting practices could be encouraging their longevity.

Is there a solution? Yes! If Real Foods were to account for the loss in profit—$120,000 in this case—as a marketing spend, I think they may see it differently. Around 10 such promotions in a year would cost about $1.2 million, a significant portion of the company's marketing spend. Would they still spend it?

So if promotions don't work, what does? Good advertising, powered by consumer insights.

In his landmark study (Jones, 1995), marketing guru John Philip Jones showed that the average sales growth experienced in the first week of advertising was 24 per cent (refer to Figure 11.2). The best brands—that is, those in the top 10 per cent—showed a 136 per cent growth in sales. Jones explained why the brands in the bottom quintile showed a decline of 27 per cent in sales:

> I do not believe that these advertisements at the bottom end actually cause sales to go down because they are so positively awful. The better explanation is that the advertising is not strong enough to protect the brands from the more

powerful campaigns of the competition when the brand and the competition are advertised at the same time.

Figure 11.2 Immediate Sales Impact of Advertising (In the First Week after Advertising)

Quintile (%)	Sales impact (+/-%)
Top quintile	+136%
Ninth	+64%
Eighth	+39%
Seventh	+21%
Sixth	+16%
Fifth	+8%
Fourth	+3%
Third	-3%
Second	-11%
Bottom	-27%
Average	**+24%**

Source: John Philip Jones (1995); *When Ads Work: New Proof That Advertising Triggers Sales.*

In other words, creativity matters. Good advertising, which is relevant, likeable, and visually arresting, helps elevate a brand subtly in the consumer's memory.

And a brand can develop such advertising by basing it on a good insight. The role of insight-driven advertising is particularly vital to connect with today's ESCAPE-ing consumer.

SUMMARY

- Short-term promotions, especially price discounts, do not help brands grow sales in the long-term. While they may temporarily generate sales spikes, they do little to lift the base sales trend.
- Further, short-term promotions erode profits.
- Good advertising—relevant, visual, and likeable—can impel long-term growth by helping the brand increase its mental availability with consumers. Such good advertising is based on strong insights.

Chapter 12
The Craft of CRAFT: A Five-pronged Model

'We are all apprentices in a craft where no one ever becomes a master.'
—Ernest Hemingway

19 May 2013 was a significant day in the annals of football—Sir Alex Ferguson retired as manager of the English football club Manchester United after 26 years at the helm. Under his leadership, Manchester United won 13 English Premier League titles—including thrice in a row twice—five Football Association (FA) Cups, four League Cups, two Champions League crowns, and one International Federation of Association Football (FIFA) Club World Cup (Elberse and Dye, 2012). Overall the club won 895 out of the 1,500 matches it played under Ferguson—an impressive winning percentage of almost 60 per cent. No football manager in the history of this beautiful game has had sustained success anywhere close to this.

Therefore, when Ferguson finally retired it is safe to assume that millions of fans were devastated . . . and terrified. Would the new coach be able to maintain the momentum?

Their fears were justified. The new manager, David Moyes, was a disaster. Under his leadership, which lasted all of 10 months, the club went from champions to seventh in the league—their worst position in 24 seasons. This was despite the fact that the team that played under Moyes was virtually the same one that had been playing under Ferguson when he retired.

There were a number of factors that made Manchester United so successful in the Ferguson years.

Ferguson came with the right **foundation** to succeed. In his youth, he had been a professional football player himself. While he never attained the star status of some of those he trained, he enjoyed a moderately successful career and was a prolific goal scorer. During his three years at Rangers, he learnt what it was that made a club tick.

Ferguson was a master in putting together the right team—that is, harnessing **resources** perfectly. He revived youth football, a founding heritage of Manchester United that had been neglected in the years before he took over. The backbone of his most successful team, which won the historic 1999 treble, was six youngsters who had made their debut under Ferguson. Their introduction was met with scepticism, especially as they replaced experienced, successful players. BBC football analyst Alan Hansen proclaimed, 'You can't win anything with kids.' The team went on to win the league in five of the next six seasons.

If Ferguson injected fresh talent cleverly, he was equally astute with letting players go. For example, when he felt David Beckham—a founding 'youth' member and an iconic player for the club—was hampering the club's performance, he sold him to Real Madrid.

Underlying all these moves was a strong **conviction** in his ability to pick the right players to retain or let go, and in his ability to train his team.

Which brings us to another important factor in Ferguson's success—his **approach** to developing a world-class football club. Ferguson's first task was, in his own words, 'to put an end to Manchester United's reputation of being almost as much a social club as a football club'. He initiated a regimen of rigorous training to ensure that the top stars stayed on top of their game. 'I tell them that hard work is a talent too,' he said. 'And if they can no longer bring the discipline that we ask for here at

United, they are out.' Over the years, Ferguson successfully adapted to the scientific advances in the sport (installing, for example, a new Vitamin D machine in the players' dressing room) and brought in many more back room staff to help with training.

Above all, Ferguson was a charismatic leader—at once passionate and belligerent, caring and considerate—a man who inspired **teamwork**. His manner of motivating his team is now the stuff of legend. He took team-talks seriously ('I like to tell different stories, and use my imagination.'). He drew from everything he was exposed to—including, on one occasion, an opera he had watched, which revealed to him the value of coordination and teamwork. At the same time, he understood that not every game required a rousing speech. For instance, before a relatively easy match against Tottenham, the United captain Roy Keane recounts how Ferguson uttered just three words: 'Lads, it's Tottenham'. Through his leadership, Ferguson earned the deepest respect from the club's whole fraternity, and the broader Manchester United 'team'—its owners, the support staff, the media and the legion of fans intimately involved with the club's every moment, be it triumph or ignominy.

What is the bearing of this football story in a book about creative excellence? First, football is not the most popular game in the world by accident. FIFA estimates that 2.2 billion people tuned in to watch at least a part of the 2010 World Cup, and one in 25 people plays the game regularly. Requiring just a ball (and a flat ground), it is the simplest form of elegance, art, and teamwork in any field—and for that reason, it can teach lessons for life's more complicated ventures.

Second, the success of Manchester United under Alex Ferguson's stewardship is famous not only in football and sporting circles, but also in business and leadership fora. It has inspired Anita Elberse and Tom Dye to write the Harvard Business School case study: 'Sir Alex Ferguson: Managing Manchester United'. Much of the material for this chapter has, in fact, been taken from here (Elberse and Dye, 2012).

Third, the elements of Ferguson's success form the basis of CRAFT (see Figure 12.1)

Figure 12.1 Mastering Creative: The CRAFT

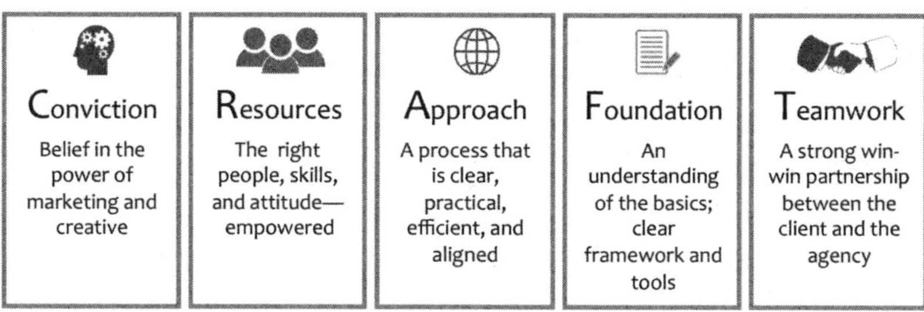

Conviction
Belief in the power of marketing and creative
Resources
The right people, skills, and attitude—empowered
Approach
A process that is clear, practical, efficient, and aligned
Foundation
An understanding of the basics; clear framework and tools
Teamwork
A strong win-win partnership between the client and the agency

CRAFT is a model based on observing tall leaders like Sir Alex Ferguson, as well as successful organizations. What does it stand for? Put simply:

Conviction: Belief is the beginning. Without it, the rest is of little use. One needs to inculcate a sense of optimism and belief in the power of insights and brilliant advertising to grow sales.

Approach: This covers the process and principles associated with good creative development.

Foundation: Here are the basic building blocks of great creative, beginning with a powerful insight (which we learnt to develop in Part 2).

Teamwork: While belief is the beginning, without teamwork, creative development falls apart. The partnership between client and agency is vital to the creative development process.

Resources: The right leadership, working with an empowered team that has the appropriate skills, can raise the creative quality of a brand's advertising to world-class.

While CRAFT is undoubtedly a neat acronym, the chapters that follow (and the next example!) will carry the slightly different sequence listed above—CAFTR, if you will.

Let's consider an organization that has benefited from CRAFT—P&G—the company that is widely credited with inventing modern brand management and is known for marketing excellence.

P&G and CRAFT

Having worked at P&G for 13 enjoyable years, I can say with confidence that if there is one defining culture that permeates the company, it is a fundamental belief in the power of great creative to build the business and enhance brand image. This belief is so strong that, for many years, the department was called 'advertising', not 'marketing'. New hires would initially be confused to learn that their brand manager reported into the advertising manager—a title normally associated with advertising agencies. (P&G eventually changed the department name to 'marketing' because it realized that the word 'advertising' represented only a part—albeit an important one—of the marketing role.)

The question in P&G was never: can good creative build sales? Rather the questions were: how much sales can this creative build? And which creative does it better? Consequently, P&G developed a very sophisticated method of pre-testing creative campaigns. Each advertisement at P&G goes through a quantitative pre-testing protocol and must get a minimum score (established through rigorous benchmarking—correlating the ad's test scores with in-market sales results) before it is allowed to be released to consumers. The fact that this is diligently followed highlights P&G's strong **conviction** in the power of its approach.

Speaking of **approach**, P&G has laid this out formally—from project inception to final advertising-on-air. Adequate time is granted to every stage. (While there are exigencies when creative is needed 'in a hurry', these are understood to be exceptions.)

Each creative task starts with consumer understanding, a clear articulation of the challenge, and a concise creative brief. Then, there is a prescribed technique of evaluating creative and giving feedback—when the agency is ready with its idea, a formal meeting is held with the full brand team. The assistant brand managers give their feedback on the creative being presented, followed by the brand manager. The marketing director then weighs in with the 'final verdict', incorporating feedback from the others while making the appropriate decisions. By following this bottoms-up process, the P&G system not only encourages juniors to give their true opinion—without being influenced by a senior colleague who has already spoken—but also ensures that the final decision is taken by the seasoned marketing director. In some situations (for example, when there are many people, multiple issues, and perhaps diverse points of view), the P&G folks may call for a 'huddle', requesting the agency people to leave the room so they can thrash out the issues without giving muddled messages; they then invite the agency back in for consolidated feedback. Once an advertisement emerges, it goes through the quantitative pre-testing protocol mentioned earlier before it is released into the world.

Clearly, the **foundation** of marketing in P&G is strong. In fact, every brand has a clearly defined brand strategy that is consistently followed across the globe and serves as the guiding light for creative development.

The P&G creative development process is based on **teamwork**. Typically, P&G marketing executives and the agency teams work well together and produce consistently good work. One reason for this is the process I just described. Another reason is that P&G marketing executives know they are more or less married to their agency partners forever. In many companies, marketing teams have the option of firing the agency at their disposal, and the very knowledge of this tends to make marketing directors treat the agency less as a partner and more as an order-taker. But in P&G, brand-agency decisions are made globally. If a brand manager of Pantene in, say, France has an issue with the country's Grey agency, his only recourse is to escalate the issue with Grey at a regional or global level. He cannot change the agency as Grey is the global agency for Pantene, period. This is one of the many reasons why partnership and teamwork tend to be strong at P&G.

Finally, if P&G has developed superior creative, it's because it has enlisted the right **resources**—in terms of attitude and skills—

right from its new hires to its senior leaders. The organization hires people *only* at the bottom of the hierarchy. In marketing, you start as an assistant brand manager and are taught the basic principles of marketing, the P&G way—through one-on-one coaching from your brand manager and through formal training, much of it focused on creative development. So, you develop your skills and your conviction continues to strengthen as you progress in the company.

While P&G sometimes gets caught up in its rigid foundation and inflexible approach, and fails to recognize big, out-of-the-box ideas (some marketers point to this as P&G's Achilles' heel), most people would agree that emulating P&G's model will do a company or brand more good than harm!

SUMMARY

- The CRAFT model covers conviction, resources, approach, foundation, and teamwork.
- The acronym offers insights not only into the success of leaders, but also into how organizations stand to benefit by adopting this five-pronged model.
- Following the principles of CRAFT has made leaders like Sir Alex Ferguson, manager of the Manchester United Football Club for 26 years, successful.
- Marketing practitioners can learn a lot about CRAFT in action from P&G, a company totally committed to marketing and advertising.

Chapter 13
CRAFT's Conviction: The Cornerstone of Creative Excellence

'The universe is made of stories, not of atoms.'
—Muriel Rukeyser

The Thai leadership team of (the fictitious) Monogram Beauty—a multinational packaged-goods company headquartered in Phoenix, Arizona—assembled in its Bangkok office to discuss a grim situation.

Monogram Beauty was going through a tough business cycle. 28 per cent of its sales traditionally came from the Asia-Pacific region. But Thailand, which accounted for 20 per cent of the regional revenue, had sales figures in the first half of the financial year that not only failed to meet the target, but were actually lower than the figures a year ago. If profit for the first half of the year remained flat it was because Monogram Beauty Thailand had taken a small price increase on most of its products early on. But now, even that silver lining was threatening to disappear. A revised projection was the topic on the table. The mood in the meeting room was sombre.

'It's time to cut expenses,' said Ian Smith grimly. Smith, the company's finance director and an expat from Ireland, almost always spoke grimly.

Everyone nodded, matching Smith's cheerlessness. After the finance director outlined the revised targets for travel and other administration expenses, he turned to Busarakham Punyorathai, the marketing director.

'Ming,' he said, addressing her by the nickname everyone used, 'you need to cut your marketing budget by 10 per cent.' She began to speak, but he cut her short, 'I'm sorry but marketing is a cost, and my job right now is to cut costs!'

'I can't cut 10 per cent of the budget for the rest of the year, Ian,' replied Ming. 'The marketing plan . . .'

Smith interrupted: 'You misunderstand me. I mean you have to cut the *full year* budget by 10 per cent. That's how much our annual projection is behind plan. Since you've spent 60 per cent of your budget already, it actually means you have to cut—let me see . . .' He punched a few numbers in the calculator and looked up with a trace of glee, '. . . 25 per cent of the budget for the rest of the year.'

Ming was in shock. 'But Ian . . .' she began and was interrupted again, this time by the managing director, Erik Wallace.

'Sorry, Ming,' he said. 'The business is down; we have to cut the marketing budget.'

'Especially today,' said Kang-Dae Kim, the Korean sales director, 'when people don't even watch television but are glued to their computers and cell phones all the time.'

A murmur of assent went around the room. Everyone seemed to agree that the digital revolution was making marketing redundant. A couple of people related personal anecdotes about how today's consumers were impervious to traditional marketing efforts; others nodded sagely.

A few minutes later, Erik Wallace summarized the room's sentiment. 'What we're all saying is that marketing and creative excellence hardly matter in today's digital world.' He turned to the finance director. 'Okay, Ian, what's next on your cost-cutting proposal?'

Immediately after the meeting ended, Ming called her advertising agency and spoke to the account lead, Kraisak Vejjavaidya. She explained the dire financial situation. 'We have to drop the brand campaign planned for the last quarter,' she said, 'and replace it with a campaign for a new buy-one-get-one-free promotion for our lead shampoo brand Velveteen.' She continued quickly before Vejjavaidya could protest, because there was more bleak news to share. 'Since the promotion campaign will require much fewer resources and less time than a brand campaign, I will need you to cut 25 per cent off the creative budget for the rest of the year.'

As expected, Vejjavaidya first argued about the need for the brand campaign. When he realized he could make no headway on that front, he said, 'Okay we'll replace the brand campaign with the promotion campaign. But we'll need the same budget for it, Ming. Creativity is an art, not a science. You can't arbitrarily assume that this campaign will require fewer resources.'

'Actually I've already done it,' said Ming bluntly. 'If you cannot work within the revised budget, tell me. I'll get my brand manager to write the creative on her own. After all it's a simple "buy-while-stocks-last" communication. We don't really need an agency to write the copy.'

While this is fictitious narrative, I've seen it play out on numerous occasions in many companies. In fact, Philip Kotler of Kotler Marketing Group and John A. Caslione of Andrew-Ward International, Inc conclude that when faced with hard times, companies quickly turn to cost cutting in many areas, including 'reducing their marketing budgets substantially' (Kotler and Caslione, 2009).

I want to pause here and highlight a few telling statements made by the actors in the above drama (see Figure 13.1). These words, perhaps with variations of language and style, epitomize the malaise in much of the business world—a lack of conviction in the power of marketing and advertising.

Figure 13.1 Typical Statements from Business Leaders

Leader	Statement
Finance Director	'Marketing is a cost, and my job is to cut costs!'
Managing Director	'The business is down; we have to cut the marketing budget.'
Marketing Director	'I need you (the creative agency) to cut 25 per cent off the creative budget.'
	'We need to drop the brand campaign planned . . . and replace it with a campaign for a new BOGOF promotion.'
	'If you (the creative agency) cannot do it . . . I'll get my brand manager to write the creative on her own.'
Creative Agency Account Lead	'Creativity is an art, not a science.'
Management	'Marketing and creative excellence hardly matter in today's digital world.'

When I ask managing directors, CEOs, finance heads and marketing leaders why they make these statements, I hear variations of a similar theme, which can be summarized in the following statement: 'Great creative? It's nice to have when the business is doing well but on a day-to-day basis, we need hard-hitting, sales-inducing advertisements.'

One reason for this perception is that people haven't seen hard evidence of advertising's potential to generate sales growth. But the fact is such evidence can be obtained by investing in measuring the return on investment (ROI) of marketing programmes. Many agencies offer this analysis—at a fee, of course.

Marketing ROI is based on mathematically analyzing all potential influencers of sales—not only the marketing spend but also external factors like the economy, competitive activity, weather, positive and negative publicity, and so on—and then calculating the incremental sales generated by marketing and advertising, after removing the impact of other factors. The key point to note is that this marketing ROI is measured in the short-term, that is, in the immediate 12 months following the campaign.

McDonald's conducts a marketing ROI in many of its key markets and, as I mentioned in Chapter 2, has found that good brand advertising consistently delivers a significantly higher marketing ROI than the average promotion campaign in the market.

In Chapter 11, through the fictitious example of the Jumbo Rock promotion for Real Foods, we saw how difficult it is for a short-term price-discount promotion to be profitable. And, to remind you, an extensive study of promotions across packaged goods categories (Ehrenberg, Hammond, and Goodhardt, 1994) showed clearly that short-term promotions *do not* produce any long-term sales growth. Sales after the promotion will settle roughly at the pre-promotion level.

The evidence is clear: brilliant brand advertising contributes to long-term sales growth. And ESCAPE-ing consumers will reward such creative handsomely—by 'liking' content and telling others about it (Engaging); buying the brand (Shopping); perhaps writing something positive about it in a social space (Creating); finding out more about the brand (Ascertaining); having fun with its online or app presence (Playing); and going out of the way to look for the brand's advertising because they like it and enjoy it (Entertaining).

Unfortunately, 'good brand advertising' is more difficult to achieve than 'hard-hitting promotions'. But as a marketing leader you're paid, not to do what's easy, but what builds your brand. Hopefully you now have the *conviction* to pursue this line of thought, as Dove did.

In Chapter 10, I described the insight that Dove chose—women don't consider themselves beautiful because beauty brands have assailed them with false definitions of beauty—for its 'Campaign for Real Beauty' featuring ordinary women, not models. What I did not tell you is that selling the idea internally took conviction and courage (Deighton, 2007). There was doubt and fear within Unilever that this strategy would make Dove less aspirational as a brand; that by belittling the concept of conventional beauty, Unilever would be teaching consumers to spend less on beauty products. But the Dove brand team, led by Silvia Lagnado, knew it had a winning idea. So, to get the Unilever leadership's support, the team filmed the daughters of these very executives discussing their own self-esteem concerns. Dove's advertising agency Ogilvy & Mather, a critical part of the team, turned the film into a rough ad. When the executives saw the film at a leadership off-site meeting, they were convinced that Dove was on to something big. There were still some misgivings (about how little branding, for example, was featured in the ad) but the idea got the backing it needed. The brand team went on to make the same film with teenage models enacting the 'self-esteem story' and Dove never looked back. The brand team's conviction paid off.

To end this chapter, let's revisit the comments made by the business leaders of Monogram Beauty earlier, but this time let's also chart out what business leaders *ought* to be saying (see Figure 13.2).

Figure 13.2 Statements that Business Leaders Ought to Be Making

Leader	What they said	What they ought to say
Finance Director	'Marketing is a cost, and my job is to cut costs!'	'Marketing is an investment; done right, it will grow sales!'
Managing Director	'The business is down; we have to cut the marketing budget.'	'Investment in the right marketing and creative can turn around the business.'
Marketing Director	'I need you (the creative agency) to cut 25 per cent off the creative budget.'	'I want better creative on the 25 per cent of my marketing budget going to the agency—so that my 75 per cent media spend yields more business.'
	'We need to drop the brand campaign planned . . . and replace it with a campaign for a new BOGOF promotion.'	'I want every campaign to be a brilliant one, sparkling with creativity!'
	'If you (the creative agency) cannot do it . . . I'll get my brand manager to write the creative on her own.'	'Let's discuss what you need to develop brilliant creative.'

Creative Agency Account Lead	'Creativity is an art, not a science.'	'Artists practise too! How can we, together, develop creative excellence as an ongoing skill?'
Management	'Marketing and creative excellence hardly matter in today's digital world.'	'Marketing and creativity have never been more important than today, when we need to connect with hyper-busy, digitally involved consumers.'

SUMMARY

- The first tenet of CRAFT is conviction. To make great creative campaigns, you have to first *believe* in its power to connect with consumers, increase a brand's mental availability, and nurture growth in the long-term.

Chapter 14
CRAFT's Approach: Getting the Process Right

'Creativity is intelligence having fun.'
—Albert Einstein

You may think: for something as nebulous and artistic as advertising, will a formal process not stifle creativity?

My experience: far from it! Rather, a formal process stimulates creativity. Over 50 years ago, the advertising legend James Webb Young—while writing that creative development comes with a 'method' (Young, 1960)—said:

> [. . .] the production of ideas is just as definite a process as the production of Fords; that the production of ideas, too, runs on an assembly line; that in this production the mind follows an operative technique which can be learned and controlled [. . .]

Author David Gill would agree. He states (Gill, 2013): 'Creativity is not a "talent", but a cognitive skill that can be learned and nurtured.' Further, he explains that there are five steps to creative development:

1. Inception—Understand the task at hand.
2. Incubation—Push the task out of your immediate attention.
3. Illumination—Allow an intuitive notion to reveal an inspiration.
4. Realization—Give your inspiration context and structure.
5. Verification—Analyze the result against the original objectives.

This would be especially relevant to creative writers of a campaign. They will likely go through these five steps before they come up with the spark of an idea.

In the 'real' world, Steve Jobs, one of the most creative people in the business world, understood that creative development requires a process. As CEO of Apple, Jobs revolutionized simple computing with the MacBook, reinvented touch-screen technology, and created the tablet. Arguably, he also invented the smartphones category. For him, creativity meant not getting caught up in a system, not falling into a rut. But this did not mean skipping the right approach or process. In his words, 'The system is that there is no system. That doesn't mean we don't have process. Apple is a very disciplined company and we have great processes [. . .] Process makes you more efficient.'

Apple's slogan 'Think Different' not only epitomizes Jobs' philosophy, but has also become the 'big idea' driving the business strategy of the innovative MacBook. Figure 14.1 captures this in my insight action plan template.

Figure 14.1 Apple's Insight Action Plan

Challenge	**Establish the brand in the fast-growing computing category.**
Context	**Large and growing category dominated by PCs.**
Insight	**Technology is intimidating.**
Brand Benefit	**User-friendly, well-designed, and intuitive products.**
Big Idea	**Challenge the status quo ('Think different').**
Tactics	**• An innovative product at the core • Stereotypes the main competitors • Premium pricing • Selling via its own retail outlets**

The Overall Approach to Creative Development and Execution

Creative development, in my experience, is a six-pronged process.

1. **Challenge:** Identify the business challenge—the issue that you're trying to resolve or the opportunity you want to tap into. An example of a business challenge for McDonald's could be to 'grow the weekday breakfast business by attracting office-workers.'

2. **Insight:** The second step is hopefully a familiar one to you by now—develop insights that are relevant to the challenge and can be leveraged by the brand.

3. **Creative Brief:** The next step is to write a formal brief, with the insight as its centrepiece. I will cover the method of writing a good brief in the first part of 'Foundation'.

4. **Evaluation:** The agency, led by its creative people, will come back with ideas in response to the brief. As a client, you now need to evaluate these ideas and provide feedback that will guide creative development. I'll talk about the critical process of evaluation in the second part of 'Foundation'.

5. **Execution:** This refers to planning and buying the right media vehicles to launch the creative campaign for target consumers.

6. **Measurement:** Finally, monitor results to plan the next creative campaign more effectively.

The approach is pictorially represented in Figure 14.2.

Figure 14.2 The Overall Approach to Creative Development and Execution

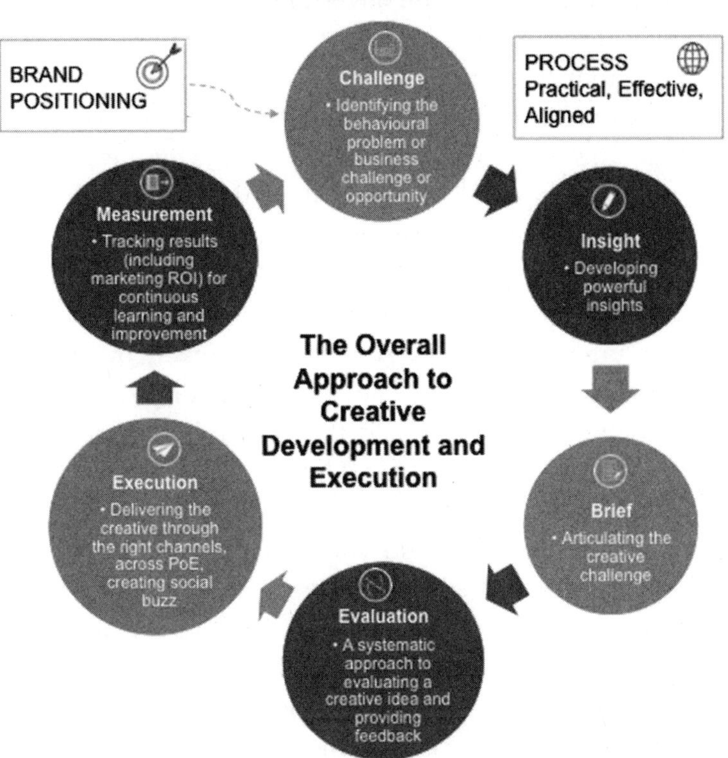

As with all templates, there can be mild variations to this process. Irrespective of the steps that are followed, there are three key principles to keep in mind.

Manage Time

A good creative development process grants the team adequate time. This may sound intuitive but you'll be surprised to know that 80 per cent of poor advertising is due to insufficient time being provided to the creative squad. In a study about what inspires great advertising, measured across over 1,000 advertising campaigns (Koslow, Sasser and Riordan, 2013), it was found that 'the more time spent on advertising development, the more creative the advertising'.

The bottom-line—provide more time!

But the exigencies of business often prevent marketing people from doing this. Here's a familiar situation: the business results of a brand are much lower than expected for the month. The current campaign is clearly not working and there is a sense of urgency—a euphemism, perhaps, for panic—among senior management staff. They discuss various short-term tactics and agree on a price-cut. They then urge the marketing director to 'execute the promotion fast to stimulate demand'. The marketing director, displaying the same sense of urgency, calls the advertising agency. 'I want the advertising to break by next Thursday!' he cries. The agency account manager puts down the phone and trots quickly to the creative department. What do you think are the chances of the creative product of this effort being great?

In this situation, the agency may ask some copywriters to work extra days and nights. If they're very lucky, they may stumble upon an inspiring idea. But if business heads don't want a campaign steered by luck, they have to give the creative desk adequate time!

A corollary: time must be balanced carefully between developing the brief and the creative. For example, if an organization spends about three months identifying the business challenge, commissioning research, interpreting the results, and using this to craft a very focused creative brief—and then devotes four weeks to get the new advertising on air—that's *not* a good balance. It's erred on the side of too much time for strategy and too little for developing the actual creative.

Hop On and Stay On

I'd urge you to view the creative development process like a boat journey across a (shark-infested) channel.

Have you ever crossed a shark-infested channel by boat? Frankly, I haven't. But I know enough about boats and sharks to understand that, for such a journey, passengers will only board at the starting point. Once the boat leaves the port, laggard passengers who wish to embark will be dissuaded either by the inconvenience of swimming some distance with luggage, or by the fear of sharks!

In the same way, everyone involved in the creative development process should join the project only in the beginning, not once the creative boat has departed from the shore.

In many companies, a senior executive like the managing director steps in to approve the final creative campaign without being involved with the process leading up to it. This is wrong. First, managing directors ought not to be involved with the creative process at all—assigning this, instead, to marketing directors. (If managing directors don't have faith in the marketing director's ability, they should focus on finding the right hire instead of taking over the job.)

But if they have to get involved, managing directors should join the creative process at the very beginning—defining the challenge, developing the insight, writing the creative brief, and so on. Only then will they have the wherewithal to review the creative idea coming from the agency.

Just as one can't board the boat once it begins its perilous journey, one can't exit it before it reaches the destination. In other words, missing a meeting in-between means missing the dialogue and agreements reached, and therefore not being able to contribute in a fair manner in the next meeting.

Therefore, everyone involved with the creative process should join it at the beginning and stay till the final creative campaign is ready.

Ensure the Process Suits Your Business

Undoubtedly, the process should fit the dynamics of your business. That is why, in Figure 14.2, I haven't recommended a specific time for each step or a specific interval in between. In P&G, I've worked on ad campaigns that have taken eight months from initiation to launch. In McDonald's, some brand campaigns have taken months to develop, but many promotion campaigns have been made within a 45-day window or less.

My recommendation is to allow at least three months from 'challenge' to 'execution'. So, if you're a 'retailer' making a campaign every month, you just need to start everything two months earlier than you presently do.

But that's just a suggestion. The only non-negotiable rule is this: please ensure you provide *sufficient time* for each activity.

SUMMARY

- Every company should follow a formal creative development process that includes:
  (1) Identifying the business challenge
  (2) Developing the insight
  (3) Writing the creative brief
  (4) Evaluating the creative idea
  (5) Executing the campaign
  (6) Measuring results (to guide the next campaign)
- For the process of creative development, there are three vital ingredients:
  (1) Manage time: You need to balance the time you provide for strategy and implementation.
  (2) Hop on and stay on: You need to be a part of the process from the beginning to the very end.
  (3) Ensure the process suits your business.

Chapter 15
CRAFT's Foundation I: Insight-driven Briefs

'You can't build a great building on a weak foundation.'
—Gordon B. Hinckley

In the previous chapter—the 'approach' in CRAFT—we saw that a good creative process covers six key components: (i) challenge; (ii) insight; (iii) creative brief; (iv) evaluation; (v) execution; and (vi) measurement. In Part Two of the book, we've covered the first two—identifying the business challenge and developing insights. Under 'Foundation', I'll talk about the next two steps—writing the creative brief and evaluating ideas in response.

Both foundation elements are important and deserve a deep look. A good creative brief can inspire great ideas from the agency, but you should be able to recognize a good idea and provide guidance to make it even better. This chapter will focus on writing the creative brief and the next on assessing ideas and giving feedback to the agency.

Starting Point: The Insight

We've seen how an insight can power brand strategy, as it did for Dove. And advertising is one of the most potent ways to bring a good insight to life in an interesting and emotionally engaging manner.

The first step to transforming an insight into a powerful campaign is by making it the centrepiece of the creative brief.

Moving on: The Creative Brief

Put simply, a creative brief is a set of instructions given to the creative agency to develop advertising.

Hallmarks

A solid creative brief comes with certain characteristics:

1. **Clarity**: A brief should explain the task without any ambiguity.

2. **Focus**: It must tell a coherent story with all the parts supporting the narrative. It should make clear choices regarding what to ask for and, equally important, what *not* to.

3. **Credibility**: The brief should be true to the brand, leveraging its strengths and honestly acknowledging its weaknesses. And in doing so, it should help the brand stand out against its competitors.

4. **Inspiration:** Remember, the ultimate target audience of the brief is the creative person in the agency who will be developing a campaign based on it. If you want an inspired campaign, make sure your brief inspires the one engaging with it!

5. **Brevity**: And finally, always keep the dictionary definition of 'brief' in mind—'short in time, duration, length, or extent'. A good creative brief should be *brief* and to the point.

The Template

Many companies have their own templates for a brief; others use the ones recommended by their agency. Some companies don't use templates at all but just write out the instructions in a free-flowing manner. And a few refuse to write briefs! Here's what I think, starting with the last point.

It's critical to write a creative brief. Unless you clearly articulate your expectations for a creative campaign, how will you evaluate it? And on what basis will you provide feedback to the agency? Some marketers sanctimoniously tell me that they evaluate campaigns as consumers—but that's nonsense. Marketers need to evaluate advertising as if their salary depends on it (which, by the way, it should), ensuring that the *best* portrayal of their brand is displayed to uninterested consumers—it should be so riveting that it stays in their memory.

It's prudent to follow a standard template to write a brief. A template is a tool to organize thoughts and get everyone on the same page efficiently, so they know what to look for in each section. A free-flowing document may come more easily to some writers, but it takes longer to digest and can potentially create misunderstandings.

While the template is a useful tool, it is only a tool. So long as it helps you write a clear and focused brief, use whichever template you're comfortable with. It's what you put into the template that counts.

With this as the background, let me introduce you to a brief template that I advocate (see Figure 15.1). You may use this for all your future creative briefs, or you could take some ideas from it and incorporate them into the template you already use.

Figure 15.1 Creative Brief Template

Goal and Business Challenge

What are the desired business results?

What consumer issue (or opportunity) are we facing?

Target Description

Describe the target that is the primary source of business.

Describe what a particular person in the target is like.

Target Evolution

How would you like to change what the target consumer thinks and does today with respect to the brand or the business challenge?

to

Insight

An emotional human revelation relevant to the category leveraged to build the brand.

Brand Proposition

Key Message

What is the key message or brand benefit?

Support

What is the evidence (if any) to support this benefit?

Tone

Describe the brand character and/or tone of voice.

Mandatory Elements

Are there any mandatory executional considerations (the fewer the better!)?

Let me explain each section here.

Goal and Business Challenge

The brief starts with the goal of the creative campaign—the desired business results that you're seeking and the source of growth.

Next to the goal, you describe the business challenge—the consumer issue or opportunity you are addressing.

Target Description

I recommend that you look at your target audience in two ways:

- Start by defining the broad target audience—that is, the people who will be the primary source of business for this campaign, or the people who ought to be exposed to the campaign. In other words, you will develop your media plan based on this target.

- Then define the narrow target audience—a detailed description of *a particular individual* in the broad target. The objective of this description is to give the creative person a good idea of the human being she should be addressing while writing copy.

Target Evolution

In this section you describe how you would like the perception of the individual you just described to change once exposed to this campaign.

First, you describe what the individual thinks, believes, and does at the present juncture (in the context of the business challenge and the brand).

Then, you describe what you would like the individual to think, believe, and do as a result of the campaign.

Insight

How do you change the perception of the target? How do you move an individual from a 'current' to a 'desired' state? Through a brand proposition that leverages a powerful consumer insight. Think of the insight as the *key* to unlocking the door to the business challenge. Hopefully, before filling in the insight, you'd have developed it by following the processes I've described earlier, working in a team with the right company and agency people.

Brand Proposition

As I've just mentioned, the insight is leveraged through the right brand proposition or promise. This consists of:

The key message—or main benefit—of your brand. Please note: I'm not saying 'key messages'. There should only be one. In case your brand's key message includes a functional and an emotional benefit, you have two choices—either focus only on the emotional benefit, or utilize the functional benefit as the stepping stone to communicating the emotional one. Here's an example: 'Rubicon fabric softener fills your clothes with the fragrance of spring and therefore uplifts your mood.'

Support for the key message. Such 'support' provides additional information that can be used if the idea requires it. Please remember: it is not mandatory for the agency creative person to use 'support'. She may well write a creative story that does not require any information from this section.

The tone—also called 'brand character' by some companies. This describes *how* you'd like to see the brand portrayed in terms of its approach and voice.

As you evaluate the agency's ideas, you should mainly look at the key message and the tone; if the agency does use the support, you should ensure it's accurate.

Mandatory Elements

Finally, provide the mandatory elements that must be seen in the campaign, to make it consistent with past initiatives and help reinforce the brand's unique heritage. When McDonald's launched its global campaign in 2003, the mandatory elements included the 'i'm lovin' it' tagline, in a particular colour and font (including starting with the small case 'i'), accompanied by five musical notes (*'ba-da-ba-ba-ba'*).

But just because the section is labelled 'mandatory', does not mean it is *mandatory* to fill the section with copious instructions! In fact, you should restrict your direction here to the critical elements of brand equity—its most distinctive assets.

Dove

We've seen how a powerful insight, as in the case of Dove, has shaped brand strategy. We've deduced the brand's insight action plan—focused on the big idea of 'championing real beauty that goes beyond "model" looks'—with multiple tactics, including the 'Self-esteem Fund', 'True Colors', 'Campaign for Real Beauty', 'Evolution', 'Sketches', and the Facebook 'Ad Makeover' (described in Chapter 10).

Unilever might have used one creative brief for all these campaigns or written tailor-made versions for each. But to demonstrate how to present a creative brief, I'm going to back-fill my own template with the Dove case study, covering all six campaigns.

Goal and Business Challenge

Goal: Achieve x per cent market share in the broad 'skin and body beauty care' category by relaunching Dove as a 'beauty brand' instead of pitching it as a 'white soap'.

Business Challenge: Dove is known as a soap (not as a beauty brand) that stands for simplicity and gentleness.

The goal clearly articulates the business objective, along with the source of growth (expansion beyond 'soap' to 'beauty'). And the business challenge describes the context while acknowledging the brand's issues.

Target Description

Source of Business: All women, across all ethnicities, of all shapes and sizes, who use mainstream beauty products.

What a Particular Person Is Like: Ann Quigg is 37 years old, married, with two children. She is a college professor, as is her husband. Ann has tried different beauty products but is dissatisfied with them—and with herself. Ann knows she's a good teacher who students look up to, but she doesn't believe she's beautiful. This makes her sad.

The broad target audience provides clarity about the 'universe' of women that Dove is targeting; it will also help Dove decide where the campaign will run (to reach this target). But, while this broad target is very helpful to the media agency, it is not of much use to the creative person in charge of writing copy.

The narrow target definition captures the insight about the false definition of beauty ingrained in women. The research described earlier about women rating themselves positively in their profession but poorly in terms of their physical attributes is reflected in Ann's description, too. Remember, we don't need to feature a woman like Ann in the campaign; instead we need the ad campaign to appeal to Ann (and women like her)—and *that's* a critical difference. In fact, the launch campaign of Dove shows teenage girls expressing a lack of confidence in their own beauty. But this would still appeal to Ann because her own insecurities probably started when she was a young girl. (There's a second insight lurking here about women's insecurities beginning in their teens.)

Target Evolution

From: 'I'm not really happy about beauty brands. They don't make me look beautiful—but that's my problem (so I use them anyway)!'

To: 'Dove gets me! The brand helps me challenge beauty stereotypes and makes me feel better about myself. I want to use Dove.'

Here is the change we want to see in how the target consumers think and behave; we want them to rethink their concept of beauty and therefore feel better about their own looks.

Insight

Reads as: Many women don't consider themselves beautiful because beauty brands—and society—have ingrained in them false definitions of beauty: size zero, blonde, flawless, toned, young, etc.

This is the centrepiece of Dove's creative brief.

Brand Proposition

Key Message: Dove champions real beauty which goes beyond 'model' looks.

Support: Self-esteem Fund—an agent of change to educate and inspire girls about a wider definition of beauty.

Tone: Provocative but empathetic—a consultant you trust.

In Dove's case, the key message is the big idea. It comes with emotional heft and encompasses all individual products. To support the cause, Dove created a 'Self-esteem Fund' that focuses on young girls, but also appeals to women because their insecurities are rooted in their teens. Finally, the tone is clear and concise. (I must iterate that this is *my deduction* of Dove's tone based on its advertising: Unilever may well have a different description.)

Mandatory Elements

I'm leaving this blank only because I'm not privy to the branding elements that Dove would require and, for the purposes of learning about creating a brief template, this is not important.

Figure 15.2 shows Dove's full creative brief.

Figure 15.2 Dove's Creative Brief

Goal and Business Challenge

What are the desired business results?

Achieve 'x' per cent market share in the broad 'skin and body beauty care' category over 'y' years by relaunching Dove as a 'beauty brand' instead pitching it as a 'white soap'

What consumer issue (or opportunity) are we facing?

Dove is known as a soap (not as a beauty brand) that stands for simplicity and gentleness.

Target Description

Describe the target that is the primary source of business.

All women, across all ethnicities, of all shapes and sizes, who use mainstream beauty products.

Describe what a particular person in the target is like.

Ann Quigg is 37 years old, married, with two children. She is a college professor, as is her husband. Ann has tried different beauty products but is dissatisfied with them—and with herself. Ann knows she is a good teacher who students look up to, but she doesn't believe she is beautiful. This makes her sad.

Target Evolution

How would you like to change what the target consumer thinks and does today (with respect to the brand, category or the business challenge)?

'I'm not really happy about beauty brands. They don't make me look beautiful—but that's my problem (so I use them anyway)!'

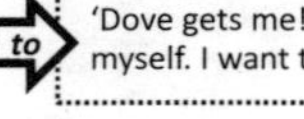

'Dove gets me! The brand helps me challenge beauty stereotypes and makes me feel better about myself. I want to use Dove.'

Insight

An emotional human revelation relevant to the category leveraged to build the brand.

Many women don't consider themselves beautiful because beauty brands (and therefore society) have assailed them with narrow (and false) definitions of beauty: size zero, blonde, flawless, toned, young, etc.

Brand Proposition

Key Message

What is the key message or brand benefit?

Dove champions real beauty which goes beyond 'model' looks.

Support

What is the evidence (if any) to support this benefit?

Self-esteem Fund: an agent of change to educate and inspire girls about a wider definition of beauty.

Tone

Describe the brand character and/or tone of voice.

Provocative but empathetic; a consultant you trust.

Mandatory Elements

Are there any mandatory executional considerations (the fewer the better!)?

—Don't know, hence left blank intentionally—

Real Foods

Dove is a great example of illustrating what an excellent creative brief looks like. But it was filled in retrospect. I'd now like to use the fictitious Real Foods to actually develop the brief.

To recap, Real Foods' challenge is developing a home delivery business. The insight we chose was 'Time is the most valuable currency for today's NOW generation.' The big idea was: 'Our food . . . at your time.'

In the insight action plan we listed these tactics:

- Guarantee 45-minute delivery, highlighted across websites, print, OOH, etc. ('$1 off for every minute's delay.')
- App to pre-order meals to be delivered at the exact time you want it (or get your money back).
- Advertising campaign on the big idea—'Our food . . . at your time'—leveraging the insight.

Let me now focus on the third tactic and illustrate how we might develop a creative brief for this campaign with my template (see Figure 15.3).

Since Real Foods is a hypothetical example, and no agency actually worked on this brief, I cannot share the actual creative campaign. But I hope you are convinced that this brief *can* inspire a powerful creative campaign, and that by following a similar process, you, too, can inspire great creative work from your agency.

Figure 15.3 Real Foods' Creative Brief

Goal and Business Challenge

What are the desired business results?

Develop the delivery business to contribute to 10 per cent of the overall sales by appealing to current Real Foods customers.

What consumer issue (or opportunity) are we facing?

Propelled by the consumers' need for convenience, the delivery market (for food and other items) is growing. Real Foods' opportunity is to become a significant player—but to succeed in this competitive scenario, it needs to be recalled easily and intuitively when consumers think about ordering food.

Target Description

Describe the target that is the primary source of business.

Young, working urban adults, 25–45 years old, who know about Real Foods and eat there.

Describe what a particular person in the target is like.

Chris Brown, a banker, and Heather, a pharma industry executive, are married; they're their early thirties and have a 6-month-old child, Christine. Their weekdays are a frantic blur. They wake up at 6 am, get themselves and the baby ready, leave home at 7.15, drop Christine at a crèche, board the 7.45 am train, get off at different stations, and, grabbing a hasty sandwich, head to their offices. Heather (or sometimes Chris) leaves office at 5.30 pm to be on time to pick up the baby at 6.30 pm from the crèche. On most evenings, they buy takeaway dinner on the way home. They hit the bed—after attending to some emails—close to midnight, exhausted. But the baby ensures they rarely get an uninterrupted night's rest.

Target Evolution

How would you like to change what the target consumer thinks and does today (with respect to the brand, category or the business challenge)?

'I like Real Foods and eat there once in a while. But I've never considered it as a home delivery option.'

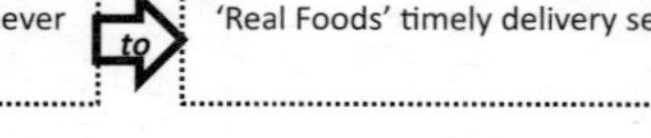

to

'Real Foods' timely delivery service is just what I need! To get food I like, at the exact time and place I want, is fantastic!'

Insight

An emotional human revelation relevant to the category leveraged to build the brand.

Time is the most valuable currency for today's NOW generation.

Brand Proposition

Key Message

What is the key message or brand benefit?

Our food . . . at your time.

Support

What is the evidence (if any) to support this benefit?

Promise of money-back (i.e., free delivery) if the food does not arrive within five minutes of the exact time of delivery.

Tone

Describe the brand character and/or tone of voice.

Witty and tongue-in-cheek humour; a cheerful friend you like to hang out with.

Mandatory Elements

Are there any mandatory executional considerations (the fewer the better!)?

Ensure the communication of exact-time delivery to establish this as the differentiating, unique service being offered by Real Foods; create and establish a visual, and perhaps also an audio, mnemonic for this feature.

SUMMARY

- A good brief should be clear, focused, credible, inspiring, and concise.
- It's not important which template you use, so long as you use one, and do it consistently.
- Ideally, a creative brief template should cover the goal and business challenge; the target customer's description; the target's evolution; the insight; the brand proposition; and mandatory elements that are integral to your brand's identity.

Chapter 16
CRAFT's Foundation II: Evaluating Ideas and Providing Feedback

'Good decisions come from experience, and experience comes from bad decisions.'
—Anon

Imagine you're a writer. You've just written a short story and have requested three friends to read it and offer feedback.

'So, what did you think?' you ask. 'Sheila, you go first; then Ram; and then Chris.'

'It was great!' Sheila says. 'But the story is a bit long. You should cut it by half. And the two main characters . . .'

'Actually, they are the only characters,' you say.

'Sure,' she replies. 'But I don't like them much. You should change their personalities drastically. And their physical features. Why is the Korean tall and thin? Koreans are rarely tall. Make him well-built and of medium height. And let the two characters meet in a bar, not at a circus. Who goes to the circus these days? Also the early part of the story is weak . . .'

After offering some more feedback, Sheila finally says, 'That's it. Other than that, everything is great.'

Ram goes next and gives an equally voluminous critique—but it's very different from Sheila's. And finally Chris gives you his independent opinion, also lengthy, also discrete.

After receiving such feedback, will you be motivated and inspired? Will you know what to improve in the story and how to go about doing this?

Your friends, though well-intentioned, probably do not know what makes a good short story—they do not have the *knowledge* to evaluate it. Second, they didn't articulate their opinion in a helpful manner—they do not know *how to provide feedback*.

We're going to focus on these two critical skills in this chapter. In the first part of 'Foundation', we saw that the insight is the centrepiece of the creative brief; similarly, the creative idea is the centrepiece of the advertising campaign recommended by the agency. In this chapter, I will cover the principles of evaluating the creative idea and providing constructive feedback to the agency. Some marketing leaders are very good at this and manage to consistently get brilliant creative from their agencies. Other marketers, who are adept at marketing strategy and business analytics, find themselves uncomfortable at the creative evaluation table—they believe creative judgement is a gift only a few are born with!

On the contrary, creative judgement is a skill that you can develop. But, like most skills, it takes practice.

The agency may present the creative idea in different forms—words, drawings, a rough video of existing footage, or a combination of these techniques. Irrespective of how the idea is presented, you should follow three simple guidelines while evaluating it and providing feedback:

1. Understand the creative idea and your gut reaction to it.
2. Use the 4E framework to evaluate the idea.
3. Follow three key principles while giving feedback.

Understand the Creative Idea and Your Gut Reaction to It

Often marketers provide feedback as soon as the agency finishes its presentation. They start with a comment (usually negative) on something that has caught their attention. For example, if an ad for a room freshener shows a couple prolonging their stay in a hotel because the room smells good, the marketer may react to the idea with this first comment: 'Why are there twin beds, not one king-sized one, in the room?'

That's *not* the kind of feedback the agency should hear first. You must start the discussion with the *creative idea* itself. Ask yourself—is there a creative idea in what you just saw? If yes, can you articulate it? In case you cannot, can the agency help? Ask them to enunciate the creative idea. If, after this, you think the idea itself isn't substantive, don't waste your time pursuing it.

Assuming there *is* a creative idea, you should record your gut reaction to it in your own mind. This is important for two reasons. One, it helps sharpen your instinct for good advertising, and over time, with practice, this instinct will get stronger. Two, while you may love an idea intuitively, you may find that it does not quite work when you formally evaluate it in the next stage. In such a situation, the correct answer may *not* be to reject the idea (I'll explain why soon).

It's equally important *not* to blurt out your gut reaction immediately. Go through the formal evaluation process, marshal your thoughts, then speak. Also if you're a part of the marketing group evaluating the idea, you should speak when it's your turn. (Here, I advocate the P&G system—start with the junior-most person in the room and go up the hierarchy.)

Use the 4E Framework to Evaluate the Idea

The 4E framework is a simple structure to evaluate creative ideas. Use it as a checklist to ensure you cover all the points in your evaluation. I've pictorially depicted the elements in Figure 16.1.

Figure 16.1 The 4E Framework to Evaluate Creative Ideas

Effectiveness	Is it on brief? • Does it address the business challenge? • Does it communicate the brand benefit? • Does it bring the insight to life? • Does it fit the brand tone/character?
Engagement	Is it interesting? • Appeal: Is it captivating, charming, delightful, pleasing? • Reaction: Will it make people think or feel differently? Or both? • Participation: Will it make people participate? Is it share-worthy?
Execute-ability	How will it come to life in the campaign? • Is it simple? • Is it fresh or unique? • Is it intelligent?
Extension	Does it have legs? • Can the idea come to life across consumer touchpoints? • Does it have longevity?

It's important for every campaign to meet the first three criteria. It should be effective—that is, it should answer the brief squarely in the way it addresses the business challenge, communicates the brand benefit, brings the insight to life, and portrays the brand in the right tone. It should be engaging—the viewer should like it and, hopefully, feel like sharing it. And it should be possible to execute it. But the last criterion—extension—is not a deal-breaker. If you believe you have stumbled on a brilliant idea but it can only be executed for a short duration or in print, you may still want to go ahead with it.

Follow Three Key Principles While Giving Feedback

Having evaluated the idea using the 4E framework, it's time to summarize your thoughts. To do so, you need to align yourself with three key principles!

1. Put yourself in the receiver's shoes.
2. Avoid the agency 'loathe list'.
3. Use the brief as a launch pad, not as a screen.

Put Yourself in the Receiver's Shoes

What do you like about *receiving* feedback? Perhaps all of this: being complimented; knowing the reason for any criticism; receiving feedback that is manageable, and not overwhelming in volume; and getting a consolidated perspective when a group is involved (rather than listening to individual contradictory views).

Now, simply apply these lessons while giving feedback to the agency.

Focus on what you like first before you criticize. However, the caveat is that you do like the overall idea. If you don't, say so unequivocally. Don't invent something positive to say. While the agency may like being complimented, it would prefer not pursuing an idea for two or three rounds before it's rejected—all because the client didn't want to sound harsh in the first meeting. Truth in this case is kindness!

Provide an objective rationale for your comments. Use the criteria in the 4E framework to guide you.

Enunciate what's most important, especially in your early comments. You can get into details and nuances after everyone has spoken and the agency has reacted to the 'big picture comments'.

Offer consolidated feedback. When you're a part of a team, ensure someone (ideally the senior-most person) sums up all the views discussed.

Avoid the Agency 'Loathe List'

What the agency loathes while receiving feedback is, in many ways, the other side of the 'dos' covered earlier, but is worth iterating. So here's the list of things you should not do:

Do not provide a laundry-list of issues. Focus on the large, strategic ideas only. Trust the agency with the executional details (like the characters, setting, time of day, and so on). If you feel strongly about some of them, bring them up after the first round of critical discussion on the strategic points.

Do not offer poorly aligned viewpoints from multiple sources. It is very disconcerting for the agency to hear that the first client does not like the idea, the second likes it but has two specific suggestions, and the third dislikes it but for reasons completely unlike the first client's—with no one summarizing the final point of view. If the agency has to choose the comment that is the most important, there's huge room for misinterpretation. Ensure that someone provides a coherent, summarized perspective.

At times, you may need a moment to thrash this out internally. If necessary, request the agency to leave the room for a few minutes. They will understand and, frankly, will prefer absorbing a single consolidated opinion, even if it is negative, to sticking around and making sense of the general pandemonium.

Do not give an opinion with no explanation. If you dislike something, you should be able to explain why. Use the 4E framework to articulate your thoughts. For example, you may say that the creative idea does not do justice to the insight in the creative brief (criterion: effectiveness); or that, while the idea is on brief (criterion: effectiveness), it is not interesting (criterion: engagement) because it's an old story that has been told umpteen times.

Do not voice a critique without clarifying if the changes needed are structural or executional. If your comment is structural, use the 4E criteria to explain yourself. If it concerns execution (the setting, characters, colours, and so on), ideally (as mentioned earlier) don't bring it up in the first meeting—and if you must, preface your remarks with something like, 'This is a comment on the execution . . .'

Do not provide instructions on how an agency must change things, instead of explaining what the issues are.

Agency creative people hate being told what to do ('Change the bicycle ride into a mountain hike'). They would rather hear what the issue is ('I don't think a bicycle ride brings out the ruggedness of our all-purpose shoes; can you think of something that does a better job?'). You may want to give an example to make your point ('. . . like a mountain hike') but don't *dictate* it. You should demonstrate the fact that you trust the agency's ability to come up with options. (Sometimes agencies can be unreasonably impervious to *any* suggestion from the client, however practical and sensible it may be. In the section on 'Teamwork', I provide some advice to the agency, too, in this regard. But for now, focus on *what* to change, not *how* to do it.)

Use the Brief as a Launch Pad, Not as a Screen

By definition, a 'launch pad' is 'an effective starting point for an enterprise or campaign'. A 'screen', on the other hand, is 'a system of checking for the presence or absence of something'.

Using the brief as a screen means checking the idea strictly against the brief and rejecting it if it doesn't address the brief well. Using it as a launch pad means encouraging an inspired idea even if it is a bit off the brief. (This, in turn, means that you're prepared to adjust the brief later.)

Now you shouldn't do this every time or even most of the time if you're doing a good job with writing the brief! But every once in a while you may come across an idea so clever, it makes you want to rethink things. In which case, go ahead and rethink!

This guideline will become clearer in the example that follows.

Synoptik

Synoptik is a brand of glasses and its campaign revolves around using Synoptik to see things more clearly. However, the creative brief is fictitious. I've written it to illustrate how ideas are to be evaluated and how feedback should be offered.

I'm assuming that Synoptik is looking for a 10 per cent growth in sales through this campaign (captured under **goal** in the creative brief) and that this is its first advertising campaign. Until now the brand has only been promoted through the optician and the point-of-sale display at the shop—this is detailed under **business challenge** in the brief.

The **target as a source of business** is broad—20- to 40-year-old adults with weak eyesight. The description of a **particular person** is Natalie Smith—31 years old; has difficulty seeing things clearly; and loathes glasses as she feels they'll make her look old and less pretty.

The **target evolution** we want is a shift in her stance from 'I look good without glasses and can manage without them!' to 'You know what, seeing things clearly is more important than looking good.'

The **insight** in the brief is: 'The world is really beautiful if only you look at it through the right lens.' (I emphasize that this is *not* the insight developed by the company.) I hope you agree it's a good insight—a human revelation relevant to the category of eyesight but also to life as a whole. As an added bonus, the wordplay—looking at things 'through the right lens'—is clever, given the category it is addressing.

The **brand proposition** is straightforward. Synoptik simply offers better eyesight, supported by its scientifically manufactured lenses. The **tone** or brand character is that of a sympathetic caregiver.

The (imaginary) brief is summarized in Figure 16.2.

Okay, now let's imagine that the agency developed the following creative idea in response to the brief:[23] A man leaves the bowling alley carrying his bowling ball. He walks to his car, parked on the crest of a steep hill. As he opens the boot to place his belongings inside, he fumbles and drops the ball. It starts rolling down the hill, gathering speed, and heads towards two men chatting at the bottom. By waving his hands in the air frantically,

23 You can watch the Synoptik ad on YouTube, at <https://www.youtube.com/watch?v=r308yCtoKOQ>, accessed on 27 December 2016.

Figure 16.2 Synoptik: Imaginary Creative Brief Summary

Goal & Business Challenge	Goal Grow sales by +10% through advertising.	Business challenge Synoptic makes high quality glasses but till now has relied on the optician for sales without building a brand with consumers.	
Target Descrip-tion	Source of business 20- to 40-year-old adults with weak eyesight.	What a particular person is like Natalie Smith, 31 years old, has difficulty seeing things clearly. But she's able to manage and is loath to get glasses; she feels they'll make her look less pretty and, more important, look and feel old.	
Target Evolution	From 'I look good without glasses and can manage without them!'	To 'You know what, seeing things clearly is more important than looking good.'	
Insight	The world is really beautiful if only you would look at it through the right lens.		
Brand Propo-sition	Benefit Synoptic glasses: the easy way to better eyesight.	Support Scientifically manufactured lenses; special material.	Tone Sympathetic caregiver.

the bowling player gets their attention. One of them waves back to assure him that he has the situation under control; he lines himself in the path of the ball, prepared to stop it. The ball hits something and bounces high in the air. The man adjusts his position and, as the ball ricochets towards him, he leaps into the air like a football player and leans back, prepared to tackle the ball with his head! The film ends just before the bowling ball strikes the man, and the caption—'Need glasses?'—appears, followed by a blank screen and the brand Synoptik.

Now let me evaluate the idea against this brief and, in doing so, follow the three guidelines just discussed.

The story is about how weak eyesight causes a man to mistake a bowling ball for something else and take a rash decision (head it!). The idea is simply, 'Weak eyesight can put you in a dangerous, even life-threatening, situation.' It's not important to phrase the idea perfectly—it is enough to simply articulate it so that it's clear.

Now what's my **gut reaction**? I love it! It graphically tells me that poor eyesight can spoil my day (I mean *really* spoil my day!). There is drama—suspense and horror build as the story hurtles to the climax and, if done well, this can be funny, quirky, and interesting.

Having silently recorded my gut reaction, let me move to evaluating the idea using the **4E framework**.

I start with ***effectiveness***—evaluating the idea against the creative brief. The campaign addresses the business challenge and is targeted right. In my judgement, it will change the target's stance from, 'I look good without glasses and can manage without them!' to 'You know what, seeing things clearly is more important than looking good.' Great! But I have to say that the insight in the brief is not leveraged at all—there's nothing in the ad to suggest that the world might seem more beautiful (actually or philosophically) if looked at through the right lens. Moving to the brand proposition, the benefit does come through. Support is not used but it's not mandatory. The critical piece missing is the tone—I have to conclude that the campaign tone is *not* that of a sympathetic caregiver. So, to summarize, looking at *effectiveness* within the 4E framework:

Creative brief element	Evaluation	Rationale
Goal and Business Challenge	YES	Addresses the challenge and will achieve the goal.
Target Description	YES	Will appeal to the target.
Target Evolution	YES	Will help the target change stances.
Insight	NO	Does not capture the insight.
Brand Proposition		
• Benefit	YES	Communicates the benefit.
• Support	OKAY	Doesn't use support, but that's okay.
• Tone	NO	Not that of a sympathetic caregiver.

Moving to the second 'E', ***engagement***, I think the idea is highly engaging. I was waiting to see the story unfold, all along wondering what would happen to the ball. The drama only increases as the ball rolls. It's funny and, by stopping short of impact, it avoids becoming morbid; instead it suggests a hypothetical scenario to be avoided!

Next is ***execute-ability***, and it's clear—the idea is fresh, and can be brought to life quite easily!

Finally, how about ***extension***? Can the idea be leveraged by other media like print, radio, and outdoor? Most certainly. Can it be used for some time? Definitely! In fact, the concept of not having glasses in life-threatening situations—done in a funny manner—can be extended in many ways: for example, a woman diving into a swimming pool, not realizing it's empty! This creative idea is a hot bed for many clever executions.

At the end of the first two steps of the three-step guideline, here's where I am:

- I've understood the idea and, at a gut level, love it.
- I've found that it is not particularly effective as it misses two key elements of the brief—the insight and the tone—but it is highly engaging, can be executed, and is extendable.

It's time to **articulate my thoughts** and communicate with the agency following the **three key principles** of putting myself in the receiver's shoes; avoiding the agency 'loathe list'; and using the brief as a launch pad, not a screen.

Let me start by ***using the brief as a launch pad, not as a screen.*** I already concluded that there are two areas where the idea is off brief: (1) the insight, and (2) the tone.

The insight in the brief—'The world is really beautiful, if only you look at it through the right lens'—is not conveyed through this creative idea. But is there a different insight in the idea? There must be, if I liked it so much intuitively. I believe I can articulate it like this: 'Sometimes the difference between seeing clearly and not could be the difference between life and death.' And you know what, I like it better than the original insight. I think it holds more potential for human drama as well as humour!

Coming to the tone, it's definitely not that of a sympathetic caregiver. So what is the tone being communicated? It's closer to that of a witty, straight-shooting adviser. It matches the insight and, done tastefully, lends itself to humour.

Figure 16.3 captures the two deviations from the brief.

Figure 16.3 Hypothetical Synoptik Example: Deviations from the Brief

Heading	In the original brief	Deduced from the idea
Insight	'The world is really beautiful if only you look at it through the right lens.'	'Sometimes the difference between seeing clearly and not could be the difference between life and death.'
Tone	Sympathetic caregiver.	Witty, straight-shooting adviser.

I conclude that the idea presented by the agency leverages a strong insight, which, in fact, is better than the one in the brief. The tone adopted, while at divergence with the brief, interacts magnificently with the idea.

Should I be concerned that the creative agency deviated significantly from their mandate? No, because sometimes—as you'll see soon—such deviation is a sign of extraordinary work.

So, using the brief as a launch pad, I would say 'yes' to this idea and revise the brief accordingly (see Figure 16.4).

A word of advice: normally I would not advocate rewriting the tone—or brand character—in the brief in response to a creative idea. But this is an exceptional case since Synoptik is advertising for the first time and there is no existing tone that consumers have been exposed to. Therefore, I can choose the best tone to bring this powerful insight to life.

Now that I've used the brief as a launch pad, not as a screen, I need to give the agency feedback by ***putting myself in the receiver's shoes*** and ***avoiding the agency 'loathe list'.*** In other words, I should start with what I like before highlighting what I dislike; and I should clearly explain my points of criticism.

Here's what I would say to the agency, worded as the consolidated feedback of my whole team (to avoid repetition, I'm referring to the points I've just made at length, without repeating them tediously):

We love the idea! It's highly engaging, can be executed, and has legs for extension because <cite reasons [see above]>. *While it deviates from the brief in two areas, we actually think you've improved the brief in both areas* <explain [see above]>. *So we should go ahead with this idea after rewriting the brief* <explain the changes needed [see above]>. *We have one important word of caution, though. The campaign should always be lighthearted, staying true to the tone of voice in the revised brief. The final scene should, at all times, be a bit over-the-top and comical, without depicting actual danger.*

Go ahead, now. Employ these principles when you evaluate ideas presented by your agency, and empower them with your feedback!

Figure 16.4 Hypothetical Synoptik Brief: Rewritten

Goal & Business Challenge	**Goal** Grow comp sales by 4 per cent and QPC range units by 12 per cent through trial.	**Business challenge** The focus on new products and value over the last few years has left core menu unsupported—so 'taste' and 'liking' scores have dropped.	
Target Descrip-tion	**Source of business** 20- to -40-year-old adults with weak eyesight.	**What a particular person is like** Natalie Smith, 31 years old, has difficulty seeing things clearly. But she loathes glasses as she feels they'll make her look old and less pretty.	
Target Evolution	**From** 'I look good without glasses and can manage without them!'	**To** 'You know what, seeing things clearly is important. And I can look good in Synoptik glasses.'	
Insight	Sometimes the difference between seeing clearly and not could be the difference between life and death.		
Brand Propo-sition	**Benefit** Synoptik glasses give you better eyesight.	**Support** Scientifically manufactured lenses; special material.	**Tone** Witty, straight-shooting adviser.

SUMMARY

- To evaluate a creative presentation from the agency:
    (1) Understand the creative idea and your gut reaction to it.
    (2) Use the 4E framework to evaluate the idea—effectiveness, engagement, execute-ability, and extension.
    (3) Follow three key principles while giving feedback:
        (A) Put yourself in the receiver's shoes
        (B) Avoid the agency 'loathe list'
        (C) Use the brief as a launch pad, not as a screen
- If you love a creative idea that doesn't exactly match the brief, go ahead and buy it. But ensure you rewrite the brief to reflect the idea. And don't do this often—get the brief right the first time!

Chapter 17
CRAFT's Teamwork: The Glue That Binds

'It takes two flints to make a fire.'
—Louisa May Alcott

'Excellent! You've nailed it! Congratulations to your whole team, Alina!' announced Simon Blemish, marketing director of the consumer division of (the fictitious) Alpha Plus. He was in a good mood.

Alpha Plus is a giant multinational pharmaceutical company selling both prescription drugs and over-the-counter medicines—and Blemish was addressing his advertising agency MMQ at the final meeting for a new creative campaign they had been working on. The creative campaign would relaunch Sereeene, Alpha Plus's leading over-the-counter pain-relief drug and the pride of Blemish's portfolio. (The three 'e's in the middle are deliberate: the brand's aim is to 'sound soothing and start providing relief even before the pill is swallowed'.)

'Thank you, Simon!' said Alina King, the account head at MMQ. 'As you know, we love this idea and look forward to bringing it to life. So, will you share it with Eguchi-san and give us the go-ahead?'

Akihiko Eguchi was the managing director of Alpha Plus and Blemish's boss. Like many business heads (and indeed, people in general), Eguchi believed he had keen creative judgement and liked to exercise it.

'No, of course not!' said Blemish. 'I'll arrange a meeting for you to present the idea. Bring the whole team—let's bowl him over!'

'No!' said Eguchi two days later. Srikanth Pandey, MMQ's creative director overseeing the campaign, had just presented the idea in detail to him, with Alina adding deft touches here and there. Seated next to Eguchi was Blemish. Alina looked at him for support but he was shaking his head sorrowfully in sync with his boss's words.

'I don't mean to be critical,' said Eguchi, as he always did before proceeding to be just that. 'But the idea is very juvenile. And it lacks credibility.' After expanding on this theme for a few seconds, he turned to his marketing director. 'What do you think, Simon?'

'I agree!' Blemish said immediately. 'In fact,' he added, giving Alina a look that nicely blended gentle rebuke and puzzlement, 'I'm surprised the agency did not modify the presentation to include my comments in this area. Anyway, let me work it out with them, Eguchi-san. We'll come back to you.'

*

Later that week, the MMQ team was in another meeting with another client, presenting their ideas in response to a brief everyone was excited about for Whistle, a (fictitious) brand of pet food. The broad target was all pet owners but the creative target was 'a childless couple in their forties or fifties who dote on their dog like a child'. The insight was: 'For many people, a pet is like the child they never had.'

'The creative idea is: "It's a child . . . no, it's a pet!"' said Srikanth. 'We want to address the insight directly by leading the viewer to believe that the object of affection is a child—only to discover, at the end of the ad, that it's a pet. The situations will be endearing and funny, and we want to have a series of them on television, in print, online, and so on. Here's one such situation to illustrate the point. And if you like the idea, we will come up with the others. It starts at a busy airport where . . .'

'I love it!' said Pierre Durant, once Srikanth finished making his pitch. Durant, the passionate French brand manager for Whistle, enjoyed the creative development process and got enthusiastically involved every time. 'Yes,' he continued, 'the idea is great and I approve of the situation, too. I'm also with you on coming up with several situations to use in rotation, across media, and over a period of time. And as you were describing the first situation, another one sprang to my mind. It features a couple doing what all new parents do—boring their friends gathered around them with detailed descriptions of their miraculous child captured in the photo album. The guests are obviously bored but are too polite to show anything but avid interest. The ad focuses on them stifling yawns and manufacturing smiles as the couple drones on and on . . . till the very end, when we zoom into the open photo album, and see that they have been describing their dog!'

Durant looked up with excitement. 'How about that?!' he continued. 'It's bang on your idea, addresses the insight directly, but in a lighthearted way without getting mushy. Could you explore that as one of the stories?'

Alina smiled. She liked the idea and was about to say so.

But Srikanth was quicker to speak. 'It's an interesting idea, Pierre,' he said. Alina sighed. She knew that when Srikanth said that the client's idea was 'interesting', he really meant it was 'stupid'. 'But it won't work. The brand will come through as frivolous and hard-hearted.'

'Why?' asked Durant.

Srikanth seemed taken aback by the question. 'Er . . . because the idea of people having an album to show off their pets is a bit absurd and . . .'

'But that's your idea! When you said, "It's a child . . . no, it's a pet!" this just sprang into my head.'

'That is our creative idea, Pierre,' said Srikanth. 'But your execution won't work. Leave it to us. We will come up with many stories that you will love, don't worry.'

'I'm sure you will,' said Durant. 'I already liked the one you presented. But I still don't understand why mine won't work and why you can't include it among the many we will use.'

'Because it's been done before!' said Srikanth, switching gear. 'Now I realize why I was intuitively uncomfortable with it. I saw an ad recently depicting a middle-aged couple showing pictures to their friends. We can't repeat that idea.'

'What were the pictures of? A kid? Or a pet?' asked Durant.

'Neither. They were pictures of their recent holiday to Italy.'

'And was the ad for another brand of pet food?'

'No. It was for a camera manufactured and distributed in Thailand.'

'So you want us to avoid an idea that has been used on a different product in another country depicting a different situation?' said Durant.

'It's just too close to our idea, Pierre,' said Srikanth, cementing the position he had taken. 'Please leave idea-generation to us. We'll be back in a week with something great.'

★

While these stories may be fictitious, I must assure you that such client-agency meetings—marked by a lack of partnership—happen all the time!

The first scenario depicts the client who abdicates all responsibility from the creative product the moment he encounters internal resistance from his management. Instead of defending the idea he loves, he attacks the agency, sometimes even contradicting himself to prove that he agrees with his manager.

Why is this wrong? First, it undermines the trust the agency has in the client and dilutes the partnership. Second, and more importantly, it spawns mediocre creative. Managing directors are most likely not experts in advertising. So, when they kill an idea that the marketing and agency teams have enthusiastically embraced, it's likely that they're destroying something good, perhaps brilliant even. And if they replace this with an idea of their own (as they often do), it's even more likely that it will be a very pedestrian campaign.

In the second example, we see an arrogant creative agency head who will not even listen to the client's idea, however good it may be. If I've met many clients who abdicate responsibility, I've met an equal number of creative heads who display maddening obstinacy—refusing to accept the possibility that a brand manager, who is passionate about a brand and probably thinks about little else, might perhaps have a creative idea worth exploring! The impact is the same—the trust between the client and the agency is undermined, and brilliant creative gets forestalled.

(By the way, Srikanth picked a creative person's favourite excuse for rejecting a client's idea: that it has been done before. But the fact is that if you widen your search and are flexible with your interpretation, you can usually conclude that *every idea* has been done before.)

Keeping these two examples of poor partnership in mind, let me describe the four key elements that make a win-win partnership between client and agency: trust, respect, attitude ('we're in it together'), and friendship.

Trust

Trust and respect form the bedrock of any relationship.

Let me start with what trust means for the **client**. The client must *truly* believe in the agency's ability to deliver world-class creative. As a client, you should do your research and look up the agency, in particular the creative people working on your brand. Familiarize yourself with their work. This is not complex or time-consuming. Simply ask the agency to show you its best work; the agency will happily oblige *and* think highly of you for asking!

Once you've seen the best from the agency, you should expect—even demand—that kind of creativity for your brand. And believe that you can get it.

So what is the behaviour exhibited by clients who trust their agency?

- When presented with many ideas, they ask for the agency's point of view and recommendations.

- They don't reject an offbeat idea outright; instead they ask the agency to explain why they think this is a good idea. (And they listen objectively to the explanation.)
- When unhappy with an idea that the agency is pushing strongly, they sometimes say, 'I'm not sure about this but if you think it's great, I'll go with it because I trust you.'
- They recognize the awards the agency gets, even those not associated with their brand.

Trust, like everything in a partnership, is a two-way affair. So let me talk about the **agency** now. For the agency, trust means believing in the client and, above all, in the brand itself. The last thing one wants is a creative head who is cynical about the brand he's writing copy for.

Here is the behaviour exhibited by agencies who trust their clients:

- They use the brand! And they advocate it to their family and friends.
- They get involved with consumer research—attending qualitative research sessions and reading reports to understand the audience.
- Much like the brand manager, they understand the business goals, the brand strategy, and the rationale behind it.

Respect

There can be no effective partnership without mutual respect.

For **clients**, mutual respect starts with appreciating that the agency is the expert in all things creative, and reflecting this when they evaluate ideas and provide feedback. Here's what clients do when they hold the agency in high esteem:

- They focus on strategy, not execution. When evaluating a creative idea, they tell the agency what they like and why. They don't say, 'I love the idea! But why use an Alsatian dog? And why is this set against a white background? And why . . .'
- They defer to the agency's thoughts on creative matters and utilize the 4E framework to guide their comments.

- They are flexible in their approach to seeing ideas. For example, if the agency wishes to put together a rough-cut film to depict an idea, they agree.
- They listen to and seriously consider other brand building ideas from the agency not directly related to the creative campaign in question because they respect the agency's commitment to the brand.

And here's what **agencies** do if they trust their clients:

- They buy into the client's business plan and brand strategy.
- When a client suggests a creative idea, they don't immediately say, 'Interesting idea, but . . .' and proceed to explain why it just won't work. Instead, they listen to it as though it were from their own stable, remain prepared to acknowledge it if it's good, and then proceed to work on it with sincerity.

Attitude

The third characteristic of a good partnership is an attitude that fosters teamwork—one that conveys, 'We're in this together.' After all, developing brilliant creative that grows sales and builds a positive brand image is a common goal.

Here's how **clients** with the right attitude behave:

- Once they like an idea, they fight for it within their organization as if it were their own creation.
- If their managers don't like an idea they favour, they don't leave the agency in the lurch. Instead they defend the idea vigorously.
- They attend as many of the downstream meetings with producers as they can and, where film shooting is required, attend a few of these sessions too. They do this to demonstrate their involvement, not to interfere with the production.

And here's how **agencies** with the right attitude behave:

- They participate in all the qualitative research, read the reports that emerge, dive into business data, and help with identifying the business challenge.
- They work with the client to arrive at the insight that will fuel brand strategy and the creative campaign.

- They write the brief with the client.
- While pushing for adequate time to develop creative they understand that sometimes the client needs something quickly to meet a business exigency (or please a demanding boss!). In such cases, they're happy to say, 'There's no brief? And you want something by Friday? Okay, I will do it (this time)!'

Friendship

Friends work well together! Recent research overwhelmingly shows that working with friends increases productivity. For example, based on a real-life study of over 170 employees, two researchers (Riordan and Griffeth, 1995) concluded that, 'Consistent with previous research [. . .] friendship opportunities are associated with increases in job satisfaction, job involvement, and organizational commitment.' Therefore a true partnership between agency and client should be steered by friendship.

What does this mean for the **client**?

- They find occasions to celebrate and build a bond. For example, after accepting a new idea and selling it internally, they might say, 'We've got management approval to proceed. Let's go out for a drink!'

The **agency** should exhibit similar behaviour.

- They should find occasions to celebrate—even if a celebration isn't warranted! For example, after a particularly disastrous meeting where an idea is shot down, they may say, 'Sorry you hated the idea. Let's go out for a drink!' All at once, a tense situation gets diffused.

SUMMARY

- A solid partnership between client and agency is critical for developing consistently good advertising and for brand building.
- The four key elements of such teamwork are trust, respect, the right attitude, and friendship.

Chapter 18
CRAFT's Resources: You Get What You Put In

'You must be the change you wish to see in the world.'
—Mohandas K. Gandhi

Who do you think is more responsible for great (or poor) advertising—the agency or the client?

Having just read a chapter on 'teamwork', you'll be tempted to say, 'Both'. But I need you to make a choice. (And only one answer is correct.)

If you say the agency is more responsible, you're in august company. Levi Strauss & Co's President-CEO Philip Marineau felt the same way after witnessing the poor sales of Levi's Type 1 jeans in 2003, despite the strident campaign built around the brand. He blamed the agency Bartle Bogle Hegarty (BBH) for a poor ad, saying, 'It wasn't a Levi's ad' (Cuneo, 2003).

If you say the agency is more responsible, you're also likely to be in the majority. In a study of over 1,000 campaigns, researchers concluded that 'many marketers assume that if they do not get highly creative work, then it is clearly the agency's fault' (Koslow, Sasser and Riordan, 2006).

If you say the agency is more responsible, though, you're wrong! The *client* is more responsible for the quality of brand advertising. Clients get the advertising they ask for through the direction they give, the creative brief they write, the idea they pick, and the way they provide feedback to the agency. In short, clients get the advertising they deserve.

It is true that agencies sometimes come up with terrible ideas. But if clients consistently get poor work, it's their responsibility to hire the right people for their campaigns. As marketers, they are custodians of the brand and accountable for *everything* related to it—its performance, packaging, image and, of course, its advertising. Clients need to provide the right direction, recognize great (and lousy) work, and attract the best creative talent in the agency to nurture their brand. And if, despite their best efforts, they're convinced the agency is not delivering a good creative product, they should fire it and put their creative business up for a pitch.

(The pitch is an invitation by the client to a few advertising agencies to compete for the business by making a detailed presentation on why they believe they are best qualified to do the job. Agencies have a love-hate relationship with the pitch. They love it when they win, but hate the preparation that goes into the assignment—days and nights of mind-numbing work, putting together a deck, and assembling the right team to present it—with usually a heady mix of local on-the-ground experts who 'understand the market', regional people to provide 'structure and support', and global stalwarts to demonstrate 'the power of the agency's network'.)

However, a word of caution: firing the agency should be the last resort, used rarely. Clients who change agencies often are doing something wrong. Many years ago, as the regional marketing director for McDonald's, I listened to one of my markets express deep disappointment with the creative agency. 'The quality of work is terrible,' the managing director told me. He wanted to fire the agency and put the business for pitch. I was surprised to hear this because he was talking about a global agency of high repute. When I looked at the agency's performance in this particular market, I discovered that they had just won an award for being the best creative agency of the year! *Who should be firing whom?* I thought. This was obviously a case not of the agency's inability to produce great creative but of the client's inability to inspire it.

In my experience, poor creative output is *always* associated with poor client behaviour—the lack of a proper (or often, any) brief, inadequate time for creative development, no insight work, patchy creative judgement, and terrible teamwork. Good creative people usually shun such a client. When the agency has the choice of either losing a good creative person or assigning her to a different client, they are likely to choose the latter option. The client then gets weaker creative people working on the account, increasing the probability that the next idea is not great! This only worsens the situation.

Creative development, in other words, can follow either a virtuous cycle or a vicious one. This is captured elegantly in Figure 18.1.

Figure 18.1 Two Cycles of Creative Development

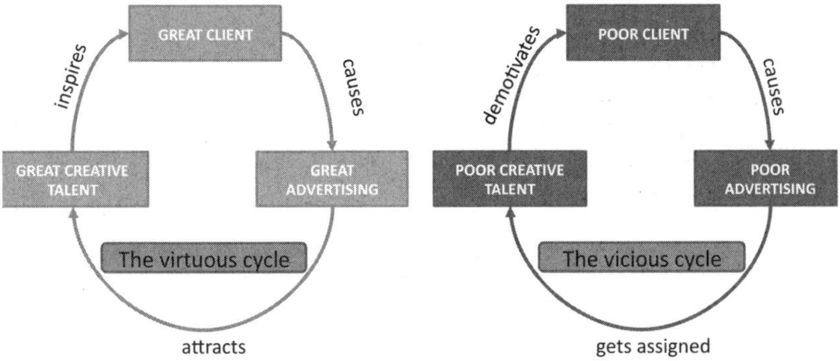

Great clients inspire great advertising. Poor clients cause poor advertising. So the secret to getting great advertising is simple—be a great client!

Traits of a Great Client

It really is simple. Here are the three traits that, in my view, make a great client.

Great Clients Display Courage and Take Responsibility

Taking responsibility for the creative means taking the final call. Most managers have an opinion on advertising; as they rise in the organization, their propensity to air their opinion only increases. The marketing director (who should provide final approval for the creative that goes on air) needs to be able to listen to these managers' opinions, weave in the relevant views, and finally take a firm decision.

It is such responsible steering that has created some of the world's finest campaigns. Take Axe, for instance. Since its birth in France in 1983, the Unilever deodorant Axe (Lynx in the UK, Ireland, and Australia) has made an emotional connection with the young male through the insight: 'Teenage boys feel awkward, shy, and overwhelmed in front of girls.' The brand sells confidence by suggesting, in a grossly exaggerated way, that the scent of Axe/ Lynx can transform everyday geeks into sexy, irresistible hunks who attract beautiful women in droves. In Unilever's words:

> Axe has become one of the world's most popular male grooming brands, by being a guy's best first move. Cool, adventurous and never dull, Axe is designed to keep guys a step ahead in the dating game.[24]

While Unilever may naturally feel chuffed about its own brand, this opinion is shared by the world at large. In an article in *Business Insider*, Kim Bhasin analyzes Axe's singleminded approach and how, despite a slew of copycats adopting the same strategy, it remains the deodorant associated with making (ordinary) guys alluring to extraordinary-looking gals (Bhasin, 2011).

The television campaign that set Axe/Lynx on this journey in the UK opens with a young, naked couple getting out of bed. They then retrace the events that had got them there—collecting individual pieces of clothing they had discarded in hasty lust and putting them back on. Their picking-clothes-and-dressing-up journey takes them all the way to the supermarket, where they collect the last items of clothing left next to their shopping carts. That's when the viewer realizes that the woman had abandoned her day's errands because of the unbridled passion she had felt on getting a whiff of the man's scent in the supermarket aisle—

24 You can read more about the brand Axe at <https://www.unilever.com/brands/our-brands/axe.html>, accessed on 30 December 2016.

he was, of course, an ordinary man who had doused himself with Axe/Lynx![25]

If you view the ad, you have to agree that saying 'yes' to launch this overtly sexual and uninhibited deodorant campaign would have taken courage. There was a risk that it would be disliked or rejected by consumers. In fact, according to Simon Clift, ex-chief marketing officer at Unilever, the marketing director did face opposition when he sought approval for what was seen as a controversial spot (Clift and Reinhard, 2011). But he took responsibility for the decision and stood by it. And his courage paid off—with this campaign, the Axe/Lynx brand flourished.

McDonald's offers a similar lesson. A few years ago, the organization wrote a brief for a global campaign to celebrate the brand. In response to the creative brief, McDonald's received one idea from each of its three creative agencies. Two were nice human stories with powerful insights; they showed simple moments of people interacting with a ubiquitous brand, and were quickly approved.

But the third idea was an oddball. It featured a young bear coming home with his school report card bearing straight 'A's. Papa bear is thrilled and declares that this calls for a McDonald's treat. In the next scene, the big, burly father bear confronts a family in the forest, having a picnic in the car, with takeaway food from McDonald's. He roars, and the family runs away in fright, leaving the food behind . . . and this becomes the McDonald's treat for the two bears to enjoy. The film ends with the dad telling his son, 'Hold on!' He picks up the car, holds it upside down and shakes it. One lone French fry pops out. As the lad devours it, dad says, 'There's always an extra fry at the bottom.'[26]

Unsurprisingly, the reaction to this idea was mixed. Some managers at McDonald's felt it was contrived, unreal, and tacky. But the marketing director in charge of the project thought it was

---

25 You can watch the Axe/Lynx ad on YouTube, at <https://www.youtube.com/watch?v=ax5U7DBDECg>, accessed on 30 December 2016.

26 You can watch the McDonald's ad on YouTube, at <https://www.youtube.com/watch?v=fKS4cfjRQ20>, accessed on 30 December 2016.

funny, quirky, and likeable. Notwithstanding the opposition, he sanctioned the advertising.

As it happened, when all three advertisements were produced and tested for consumer acceptance, the 'bear' commercial received the best approval ratings. Consumers found the story surprising and funny, and could relate to it.

Because the marketing director, at the outset, displayed courage and backed what he liked—in other words, because he refused to take the easy route of bowing to consensus—a world-class creative campaign was produced, instead of being trashed.

I hope these two examples have demonstrated how great clients take risks. They accept full responsibility for their decision, support the agency that comes up with the idea, and implement it with passion.

Great Clients Trust Their Agencies

Sometimes the agency believes very passionately in an idea but the client's reaction is tepid—or even negative. But, as we learnt in the last chapter, great clients sometimes trust the agency enough to go against their own judgement and endorse an idea that the agency feels strongly about.

Keith Reinhard, then chairman of the advertising agency DDB Worldwide, told a group of us at McDonald's about a quirky idea that DDB had come up with for Budweiser many years ago. The story unfolds in an office where the boss has installed a new rule—any time that employees use a swear word, they have to put some loose change into a 'swear jar' that sits prominently on a desk accessible to everyone. When people get to know that once the jar is full, the money will be used to buy Budweiser beer for everyone, they deliberately start swearing at each other and dropping coins into the jar so that it fills up soon! The result is an endearing, funny commercial that's shot tastefully, with every swear word bleeped out (which only adds to the humour).[27]

---

27 You can watch the Budweiser ad on YouTube, at <https://www.youtube.com/watch?v=EJJL5dxgVaM>, accessed on 30 December 2016.

When DDB presented this idea, the client was very uncomfortable with it. But the agency passionately explained how much they loved the concept and assured the client that it would be tastefully executed. So, the folks at Budweiser trusted the agency and said yes. The ad that emerged is one of the most memorable ones made for Budweiser—which, by the way, has an enviable reputation of consistently making great ads (Clift and Reinhard, 2011).

Great Clients Don't Dictate Creative Output

Marketers know their brand. They understand their consumers. Because of this, they often believe they know 'what works' on their brand from a creative point of view and have a tendency to dictate this—in terms of specific instructions—to the agency.

Great clients, however, keep this tendency in severe check. They remind themselves that they're paying a creative agency to develop the campaign because of the *creative skills* the agency brings to the table. Therefore they restrict themselves to strategic points (which I covered under 'Foundation'), focusing on what they like or dislike, and why.

Let's have some fun by imagining how a not-so-great client might react to a simple but powerful outdoor campaign for Nike (shown in Figure 18.2).

Figure 18.2 Nike Print Advertisement: Original

There is no Nike logo! The client insists that the agency insert it. The new ad may look like Figure 18.3.

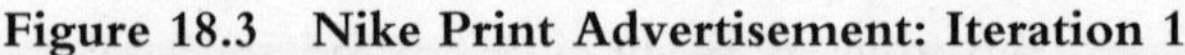

Figure 18.3 Nike Print Advertisement: Iteration 1

Now the client takes the dictating up a notch. 'Hello, what are we selling, folks?!' he asks. 'Show the product, for god's sake! And how about also showing our target audience? Using our product, maybe? And while you're at it, increase the size of the logo.' Figure 18.4 might be the result.

Figure 18.4 Nike Print Advertisement: Iteration 2

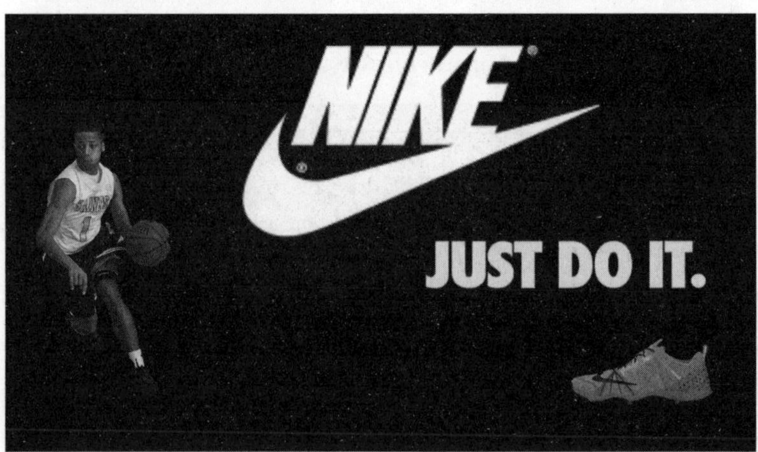

Perhaps the slogan is a bit too brief for this client. 'Mmm . . . "Just do it" is nice,' he says, 'but I want Nike in the sentence.'

The agency will respond with something like Figure 18.5.

Figure 18.5 Nike Print Advertisement: Iteration 3

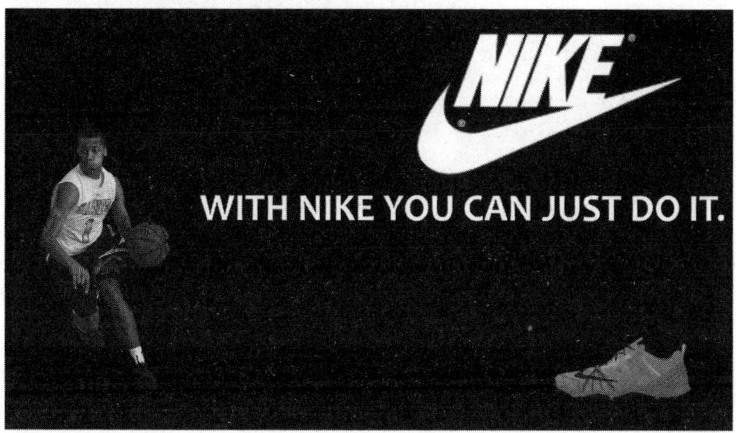

'Much better,' says the client, 'but what about the technology that goes into creating Nike shoes? We're proud of it, you know. So feature it.' Figure 18.6 might be how the agency's next submission looks.

Figure 18.6 Nike Print Advertisement: Iteration 4

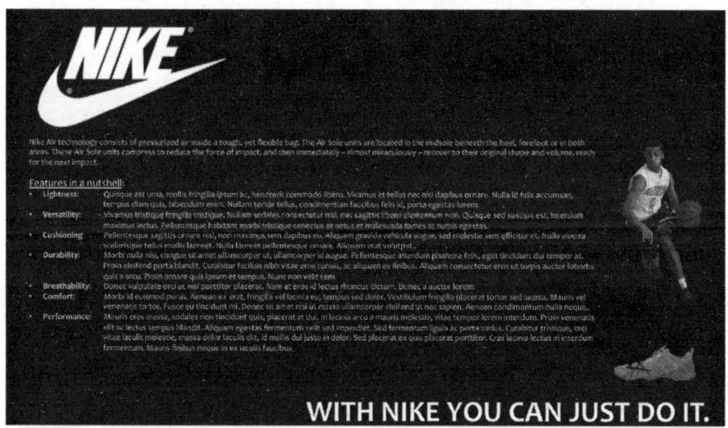

'Almost there,' says the client, smiling encouragingly. 'Now, let's drive them to the store by telling them where they can buy the product. That's what it's all about, folks!'

So at the end of this exercise, the Nike outdoor campaign may look like Figure 18.7.

Figure 18.7 Nike Print Advertisement: Final (Hypothetical) Version

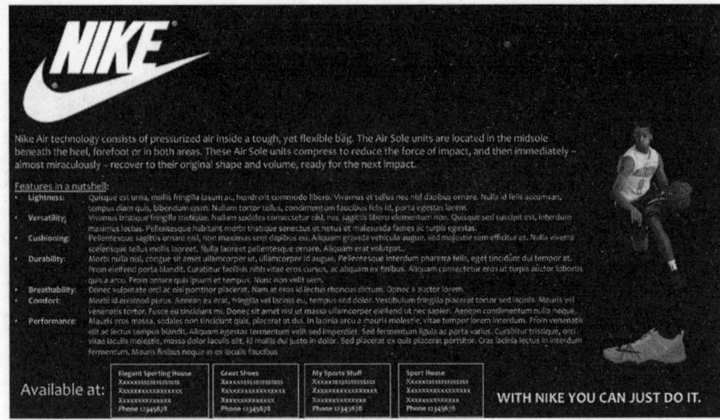

To make a clear comparison, Figure 18.8 shows the original and the final ads next to each other.

Figure 18.8 Nike Print Advertisement: Original and Final (Hypothetical) Versions

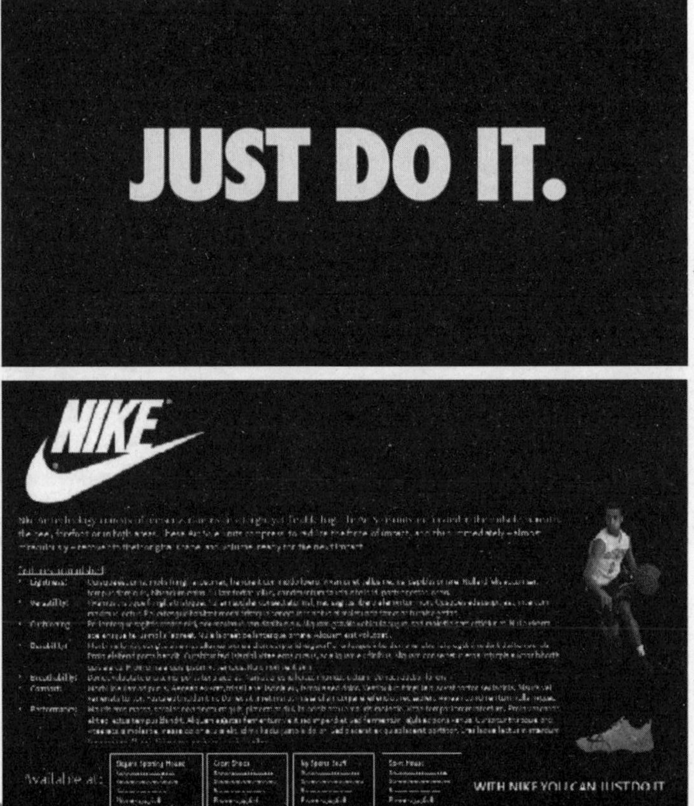

Sometimes pictures say it all.

Of course, nothing like this actually happened at Nike. (As a matter of fact, Nike is known for its wonderful advertising.)

But look around you at the actual outdoor campaigns polluting the countryside—you will see many that are like the imaginary ad depicted in Figure 18.7. And you can be sure no creative person worth his salt will come up with billboards like them—they *have to be* the result of a client dictating copy.

Great Clients and CRAFT

It is no coincidence that the qualities of a great client and CRAFT go hand in hand:

1. Great advertising is a reflection of the client's **belief and ambition**. Clients get the creative they deserve, the creative they inspire, the campaign they demand. In other words, they have the **conviction**.
2. Brilliant campaigns are linked to the client's **passion, leadership, and behaviour**. Great clients bring the right **resources** to the creative process.
3. Great clients realize the importance of adhering to a solid, practical **process of creative development**. They follow the right **approach**.
4. Great clients have the **skills** for creative development—including the ability to write a clear, inspiring brief, exhibit sound creative judgement, and provide such judgement via feedback that is constructive and motivating. Their **foundation** is strong.
5. Finally, great clients form great **partnerships** with their agency. They exhibit **teamwork**.

SUMMARY

- Clients get the advertising they deserve!
- Great clients display courage and take responsibility; trust the agency; and don't dictate the creative output.
- Great brand development is a reflection of the client's CRAFT.

Chapter 19
A Few Words in Parting

'It is not in the pursuit of happiness that we find fulfilment, it's in the happiness of pursuit.'
—Denis Waitley

Now that you've read *Spark*, I'd like to come back to why you should actively start the pursuit of insights for your brand. It's not because doing this will thrill you (though it will!), but because it is the way to grow your brand in the long-term. I've made some of these points throughout the book but by collating them here at the end in a question-and-answer format, I hope your conviction in the 'spark' that begins with the insight grows stronger.

What's the relevance of insights and advertising in today's digital marketing era?

First, what is digital marketing? In reality, 'digital' is a meaningless word when it qualifies 'marketing'.

Marketing, put simply, means satisfying consumers' needs and wants. Yes, today's ESCAPE-ing consumers are digitally connected throughout their waking life. And to reach them effectively, we have to not only find insights that are relevant to them but also ensure that we communicate through the media they use. But we don't need new nomenclature to do this!

If 'digital marketing' doesn't make sense, the term 'digital media' is equally meaningless. Tom Goodwin, senior vice president for strategy and innovation at Havas Media (Goodwin, 2014), captures this elegantly:

> There is not a more meaningless divide and obsession than the notion of digital media. Media channels were once clearly distinguished and named from the physical devices that we used to consume them. Radio ads played on radios and were audio, TV ads played on TVs and were moving images, newspaper ads were images in the paper while outdoor ads were the images around us. In 2014 the naming legacy is both misleading and of no value. I listen to the radio on my phone, read the newspapers on a laptop, watch YouTube on my TV and read magazines on my iPad. Our old media channels mean nothing yet their names survive and mislead us into artificially limited thinking. We focus endlessly on battles of no meaning like on whether digital is eating TV, rather than unleashing our minds on the new possibilities and how best to buy media and supply messages in the digital age.

Let's look at Goodwin's point through the lens of two brands I've discussed—Dove and Snickers. To address the insight that women don't feel good about their physical attributes because they're assailed by false depictions of beauty, Dove has been championing 'real beauty' *across traditional and digital channels*—television spots (like the 'True Colors' ad), billboards, print, internet, and social media. Similarly, Snickers has celebrated its key message—that when hunger makes you disagreeable, the bar transforms you to your *real you*—through a humorous television campaign. But we've seen that the brand can bring this idea to life in many other ways—like partnering with Snapchat and creating a branded filter that transforms people into disagreeable caricatures when they're hungry; sponsoring a spoof programme on 'hunger-anger management'; and using the digital medium to offer existing ads to people when they're presumably hungry (for example, alongside food reviews, recipes, and so on).

Dove and Snickers, therefore, are not performing an esoteric task called 'digital marketing'—they are simply marketing their brand to their consumers who happen to use the digital medium a lot.

Isn't television dead, or at least dying?

Television has dominated the advertising space for three good reasons—it's accessible to the largest spread of people (high reach); it offers ads with movement and sound (high impact); and it is reasonably priced (cost efficiency). (While television advertising requires a big budget, it delivers a reasonable 'cost per thousand people reached'.) Much of the growth in television advertising has come at the expense of spending on other channels, like radio.

So, it is only fitting that, if consumers are no longer watching television, marketers should forsake this medium, or reduce their spending on it. But are consumers really abandoning television?

Data from the four countries I've looked at shows that this is far from the truth. In the UK (Figure 19.1), Australia (Figure 19.2), Canada (Figure 19.3), and India (Figure 19.4) people are still watching television and for a significant amount of time. In fact, in all these nations, the number of people and the hours spent viewing TV have either stayed the same or grown slightly. (In India, the audience measurement system was changed in 2015 from TAM to the Broadcast Audience Research Council [BARC]; so data for 2015 and 2016, while available, is not strictly comparable to the preceding years' records. Nonetheless, they confirm television's high reach.)

My advice: You should assess the data for your country before you begin diverting marketing dollars away from television!

Figure 19.1 Reach and Consumption of Television in the UK

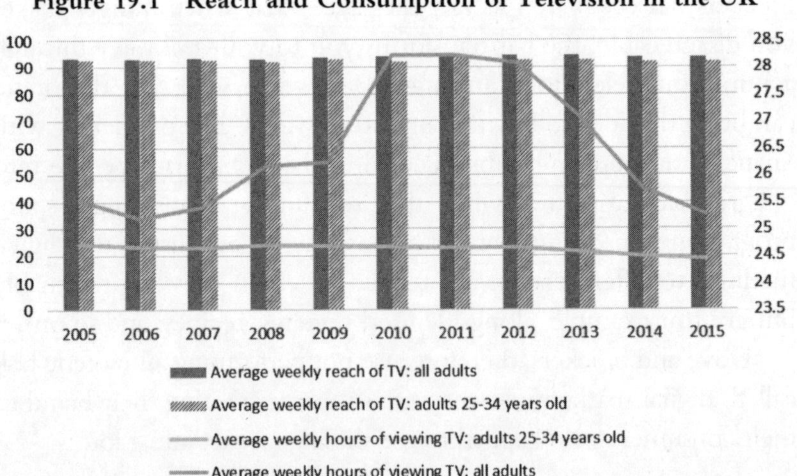

Source: Broadcasters' Audience Research Board, UK (March 2016).

Figure 19.2 Australia's Television Viewing Patterns: Average Time Spent Viewing Free-to-air Television (Number of Hours); All Consumers

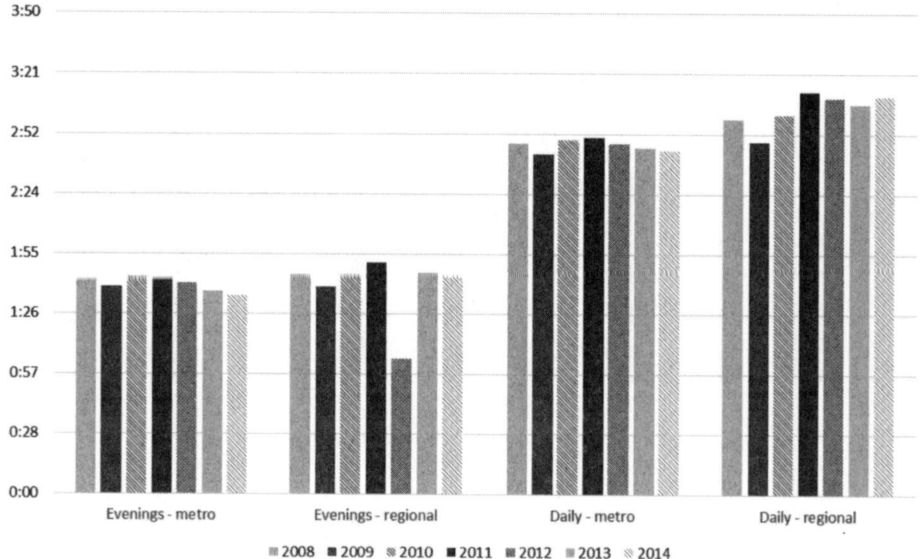

Source: Screen Australia (2014); OzTAM and RegionalTAM; 'Time Spent Viewing Free-to-air (FTA) Television, 2008-2014'.

Figure 19.3 Canada's Television Viewing Patterns:Average Time Spent Viewing Free-to-air Television (Number of Hours)

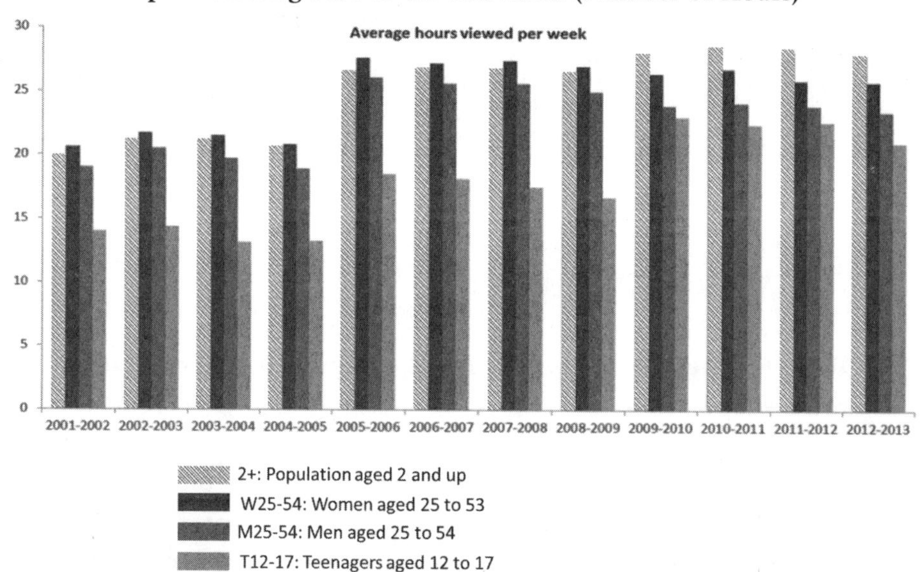

Source: The Canadian Broadcast Industry: The Landscape and How TV Is Bought in Canada (September 2014); Television Bureau of Canada (TVB).

Figure 19.4 India's Television Viewing Patterns:

A) Average Weekly Reach of Television

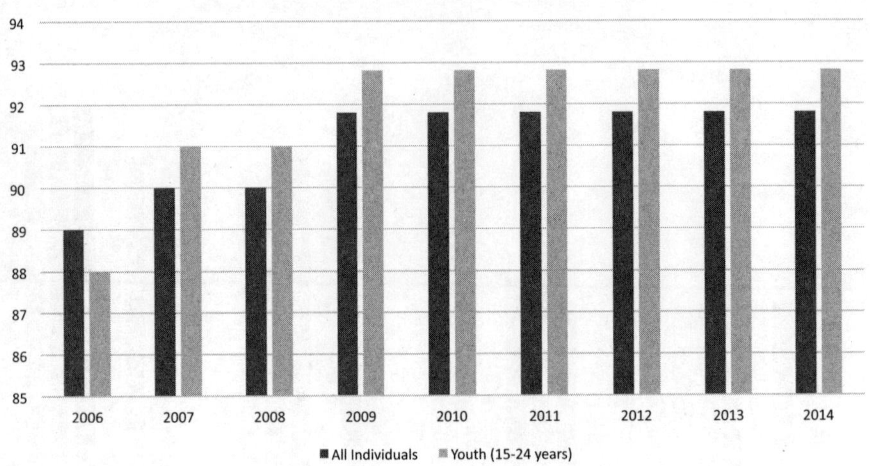

B) Average Time Spent Viewing Free-to-air Television (Number of Hours)

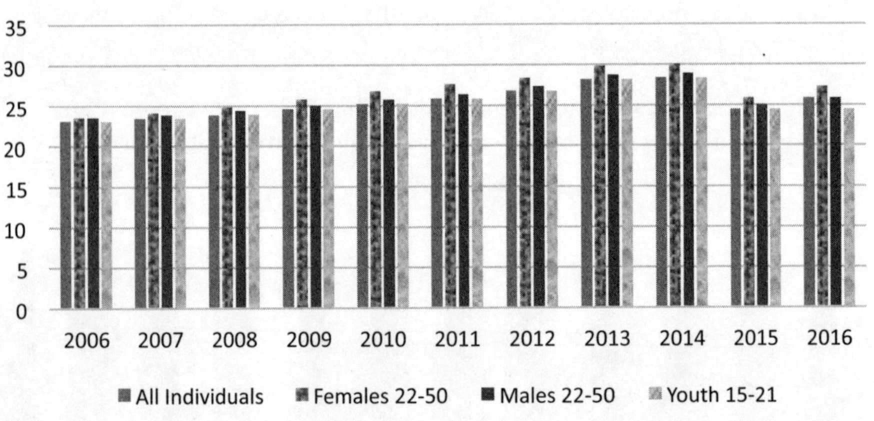

Source: TAM Media Research Data, India.

Okay, but people are watching television on other devices, aren't they?

It's true that today people do watch television on their mobile phones and computers, *but* not as much as you may think. See Figures 19.5, 19.6, and 19.7. In Australia, India, and Canada, the bulk of TV-viewing—more than 80 per cent in each country—takes place on the good old television set!

Figure 19.5 Australia's Video Viewing, Average Time Spent Per Month (Hours) (TV/PC/Smartphone/Tablet)

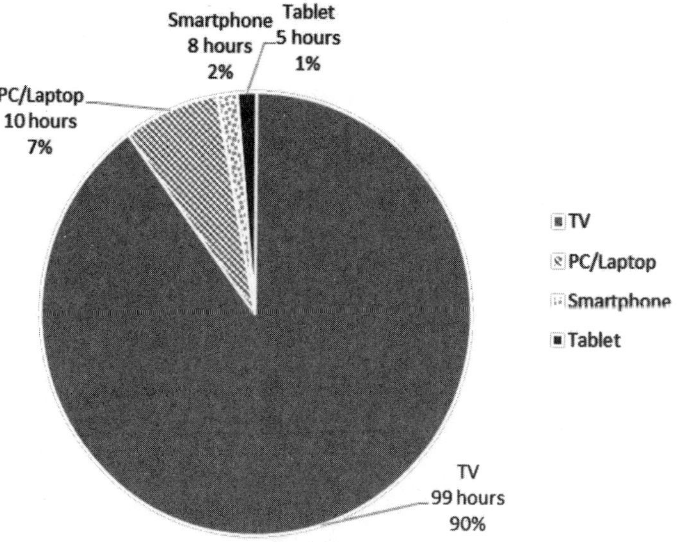

Source: Australia Multi-Screen Report Q1 (2014).

Figure 19.6 India's Video Viewing,Average Time Spent (Hours) Per Month and Percentage (TV/PC/Smartphone/Tablet)

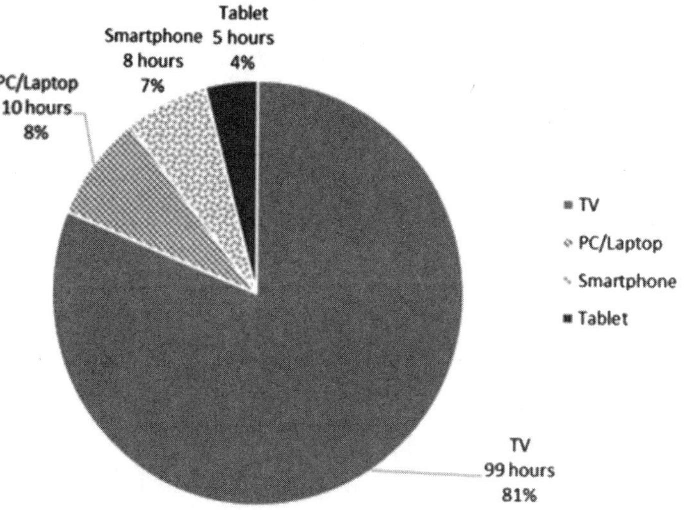

Source: TAM Media Research, India; and Broadcast Audience Research Council (BARC), India.

Figure 19.7 Canada's Video Viewing, Average Time Spent (Hours) Per Month and Percentage

(TV/PC/Smartphone/Tablet)

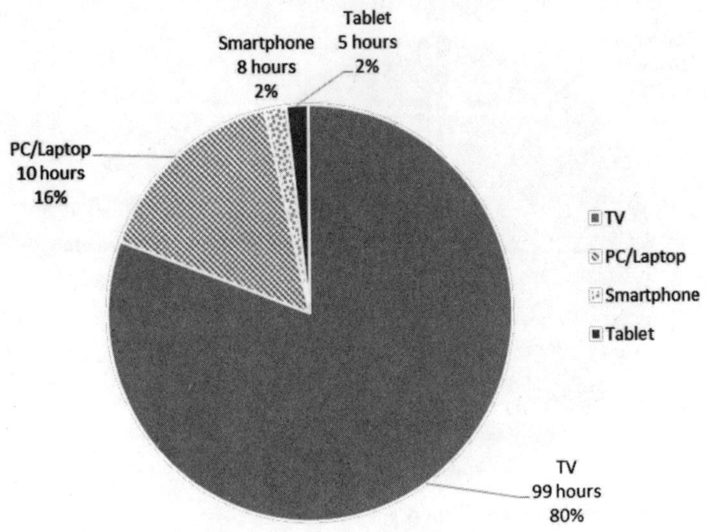

Source: Ipsos Reid MediaCT; 'The New TV Landscape: Understanding Broadcast Television Within the New Media Landscape in Canada.'

In other words, don't blindly move your marketing budget from television to other digital media without first understanding the data in your market.

But should I not spend my limited budget on my digital strategy, before getting to marketing and advertising?

'Digital strategy' is another dangerous term because, when called out separately, it often gets treated like that—as an independent plan, divorced from the overall business or marketing plan, and worked on by a separate 'digital group'.

Moving past this contention for a moment, let's look at three popular components of 'digital strategy':

1. E-commerce
2. Search engine optimization
3. App development

You should pursue the first two but not at the expense of marketing. The third *could* be a part of your marketing budget, but invest in it warily. Let me explain this further.

E-commerce is a critical area that companies should be investing in, and quickly. As more and more consumers buy online, companies need to be visible on the internet. E-commerce should be viewed exactly as modern trade was several years ago—as an essential distribution investment.

E-commerce is growing rapidly because (to use a common analogy) we're filling water in the pipes. Once the pipes are full—that is, once e-commerce is fully established, and consumers have set habits regarding the products and services they'll buy online, and the total shopping they'll do online—demand for your brand via e-commerce will be determined by marketing, or mental availability. So don't take money out of the important task of keeping your brand alive in your consumers' memory!

Search engine optimization (SEO) is also important because consumers are constantly surfing the web to learn more about products and services, how others rate them, and so on ('ascertaining' in my ESCAPE model rears its head). It is critical that your brand is easy to find. But once again, this only ensures that your brand remains physically available when consumers are looking. For prolonged mental availability, you need to invest not just in SEO but also in mass marketing.

App development is a tricky area. Consumers usually use apps that simplify day-to-day tasks like booking tickets for movies, finding the best route while driving or walking, hailing public transport, and so on. If your brand offers such a utility or service, by all means invest in an app. For example, brands like KFC and McDonald's that offer a delivery service should certainly develop an app (and indeed, have!), so consumers can conveniently place orders via it. But they shouldn't fund such a 'utility' app from the marketing budget.

However, unlike e-commerce and SEO, you *could* also pursue an app as part of your marketing programme—but do so with caution. Ensure that the idea of the app is part of your marketing strategy, and helps bring your brand proposition and insight to life. As an example, let me relate my experience building McDonald's breakfast business. The marketing target was the young working adult who realized breakfast was important but didn't have the time for it—weekday mornings were too rushed! The insight we developed was 'Not being "morning people", most adults don't look forward to weekdays.' To address this insight, the big idea we came up with was: 'Give mornings a chance.' We brought the idea to life with a range of tactics, including product innovation, improved service, smart pricing, and advertising. As part of this, we developed an app to wake people up a bit cheerfully—a morning alarm that came with a small surprise, such as free McDonald's food, or a tiny freebie from a partner brand, or simply a meaningful or humorous thought. The app (which we piloted in two markets) was a big success. Since it delivered an everyday utility (a morning alarm) within the big idea of the marketing plan ('Give mornings a chance'), it was an eminently justifiable part of the budget.

Remember, you may not always need a standalone app. Partnering with an existing popular app is a clever option, too, because it obviates the need for consumers to download yet another new app and taps into their existing usage patterns. The key is to find a fit between your big idea and the app function. For Snickers, for instance, the big idea ('Snickers transforms you back to your real you!') is a perfect fit with Snapchat's amusing feature of face morphing! Therefore, partnering with Snapchat is a far smarter option for Snickers than building its own 'face-transformation-for-fun' app.

⋆

To conclude:

- Don't think of digital marketing as something detached from general marketing. In fact, don't think of digital marketing at all. Focus, instead, on getting the attention of today's digitally-immersed, ESCAPE-ing consumers. Ensure you communicate in ways that they find relevant, and that you use the right media.

- Look carefully at the data in your market before deciding how much to advertise in traditional and digital media. Remember, media planning should be based on a no-nonsense, hard-nosed *quantitative* evaluation of reach, frequency, and cost efficiency, with the focus on your brand's target audience.
- Pursue e-commerce and SEO, but not at the expense of demand-building, insight-driven marketing, and advertising.
- Go ahead and invest in an app that delivers an everyday utility, but fund it correctly. (For example, a delivery or e-commerce app should be part of the sales or distribution budget.) Think carefully before investing in an app as a way to communicate your big idea. Partner with existing apps where it makes sense.

I leave you with these thoughts as you develop consumer insights to connect with today's digitally active, ESCAPE-ing consumer and thus increase your brand's mental availability—which is key to its growth.

The right people—from marketing, consumer insights, and the ad agency—should work on every campaign as a team. Starting with the business challenge, they should collectively employ brainstorming techniques (described in this book) to develop an insight, then *act* on it.

Insights should guide your brand strategy and your marketing plans, including the advertising. And the route to powerful advertising is CRAFT: conviction, resources, approach, foundation, and teamwork.

I hope you embark on the exciting journey of growing your brand and having fun in the process!

Acknowledgements

Writing *Spark* was an exciting adventure. I would like to thank my agent Priya Doraswamy for believing in the book and partnering with me throughout the journey. She worked tirelessly to secure the perfect publisher for the book: Simon & Schuster.

I would also like to thank my editor Dharini Bhaskar, as well as her editorial team, for the meticulous and painstaking attention she gave to the manuscript. Her input has made the book crisper, cleaner, and eminently more readable.

Finally, while I have always believed in the power of insights and emotional advertising to grow brands, I want to thank the Ehrenberg-Bass Institute for Marketing Science for cementing my conviction with hard quantitative data on the source of brand growth. The book contains many references to the work done by the institute.

Bibliography

Adweek Social Times; '79% of people 18–44 have their smartphones with them 22 hours a day'; Allison Stadd; 2013.

Bhasin, Kim; 'How Axe became the top-selling deodorant by targeting nerdy losers'; *Business Insider;* 10 October 2011.

Chokkattu, Julian and Crook, Jordan; 'A brief history of Uber'; Techcrunch.com; August 2014.

Clift, Simon and Reinhard, Keith; Discussions with the author during a McDonald's training session on creative excellence; 2011.

Cuneo, Alice Z.; 'Levi's CEO blames slow launch on spots'; *Advertising Age*; 31 March 2003.

Deighton, John A.; 'Dove: Evolution of a brand'; *Harvard Business School;* Ref #9-508-407; October 2007.

Ehrenberg, Andrew S.C., Hammond, Kathy, and Goodhardt, Gerald J.; 'The after-effects of price-related consumer promotions'; *Journal of Advertising Research;* July–Aug 1994.

Elberse, Anita and Dye, Thomas; 'Sir Alex Ferguson: Managing Manchester United'; *Harvard Business School;* Ref.: 9-513-051; 20 September 2012.

Gill, David; 'The process of creativity'; *B&T Weekly;* 30 September 2013.

Goodwin, Tom; 'Welcome to the future of advertising, where the word digital is redundant'; *The Guardian: Media and Tech Network;* 18 December 2014.

Gosling, Brent and Jathanna, Ranjit; 'OMO/Surf Excel/Breeze: Dirt is good—The value of dirt'; Warc Prize for Asian Strategy; Shortlisted; 2012.

Groves, Martha; 'Richardson-Vicks gets "White Knight" bid of $1.2 Billion from P&G'; *Los Angeles Times;* 2 October 1985.

Haidt, Jonathan; *The Righteous Mind: Why Good People are Divided by Politics and Religion*; Vintage Books; 2012.

Hansen, Benjamin; 'Punishment and deterrence: Evidence from drunk driving'; NBER Working Paper No. 20243; JEL No. I18,I28,K14,K42; June 2014.

Herrera, Carolina; 'Dove: The Campaign for Real Beauty and Dove Self-esteem Fund'; Showcase of Fundraising Innovation and Inspiration (SOFII); June 2012.

Jones, John Philip; *When Ads Work: New Proof that Advertising Triggers Sales*; Routledge; 2015.

Kahneman, Daniel; *Thinking, Fast and Slow*; Farrar, Straus and Giroux; 2011.

Koslow, Scott, Sasser, Sheila L., and Riordan, Edward A.; 'Do marketers get the advertising they need or the advertising they deserve? Agency views of how clients influence creativity'; *Journal of Advertising*; pp. 81–101; Fall 2006.

Kotler, Philip and Caslione, John A.; 'How marketers can respond to recession and turbulence'; *Journal of Customer Behaviour*; June 2009.

Leslie, Ian; 'How the mad men lost the plot'; *The Financial Times*; 6 November 2015; http://www.ft.com/intl/cms/s/2/cd1722ba-8333-11e5-8e80-1574112844fd.

Liu, Hongzuo; 'Uber offers rides in Lamborghinis, Maseratis in Singapore'; *Mobile Apps*; 26 March 2015.

Macleod, Duncan; 'NAPCAN children see children do'; *Inspiration Room*; November 2006; http://www.theinspirationroom.com.

Marr, Bernard; 'Big data: 20 mind-boggling facts everyone must read'; *Forbes*; 30 September 2015.

McGregor, Jay; 'Uber trials fast food delivery service "UberFRESH"'; *Forbes/Tech*; August 2014.

Min, Thia Shi; 'Posters of bike handlebars as hunting trophies urge road respect for cyclists'; *Taxi*; March 2014.

Olarte, Olivia; 'Human error accounts for 90% of road accidents'; *Fleet Alert Magazine* from *Alertdriving*; April 2011; http://www.alertdriving.com.

Ong, Josh; 'Uber announces UberPool, a carpooling experiment with 40% lower prices than UberX'; *TNW News*; 6 August 2014.

Proudlove, Nathan; '"Search widely, choose wisely": A proposal for linking judgemental decision-making and creative problem-solving approaches'; *Creativity and Innovation Management;* Volume 7(2); pp. 73–82; June 1998.

Ricki; 'Coca-Cola connects Indians and Pakistanis together through a live communications portal via Leo Burnett Chicago and Leo Burnett Sydney'; May 2013; http://www.campaignbrief.com.

Riordan, Christine M. and Griffeth, Rodger W.; 'The opportunity for friendship in the workplace: An underexplored construct'; *Journal of Business and Psychology;* Volume 10(2); Winter 1995.

Romaniuk, Jenni and Sharp, Byron; *How Brands Grow: Part 2*; Oxford University Press; 2016.

Romaniuk, Jenni, Sharp, Byron, and Ehrenberg, Andrew; 'Evidence concerning the importance of perceived brand differentiation'; *Australasian Marketing Journal*; Volume 15; 2007.

Rothfeld, Lindsay; '6 trends redefining the way we watch television'; *Mashable Asia*; December 2014; http://mashable.com/2014/12/23/future-of-television/#mKI7MU_eFqqj.

Salesforce Marketing Cloud; 2014 Mobile Behaviour Report; https://www.exacttarget.com/sites/exacttarget/files/deliverables/etmc-2014mobilebehaviorreport.pdf.

Saunders, Barbara M.; 'Better brainstorming'; Harvard Management Communication Letter; #C9911C; November 1999.

Sharp, Byron and the researchers of the Ehrenberg-Bass Institute; *How Brands Grow: What Marketers Don't Know*; Oxford University Press; 2010.

Terech, Andres, Bucklin, Randolph E., and Morrison, Donald G.; 'Consideration, choice and classifying loyalty'; Marketing Letters; 20.3; September 2009.

Wormeli, Rick; *Metaphors & Analogies: Power Tools for Teaching Any Subject*; Stenhouse Publishers; 2009.

Xueming, Luo and de Jong, Pieter J.; 'Does advertising spending really work? The intermediate role of analysts in the impact of advertising on firm value'; *Academy of Marketing Science Journal*; 40.4; pp. 605-624; July 2012.

Young, James Webb; 'A technique for producing ideas'; Crain Communications; 1940.